100 TIPS FOR
Traveling with Kids in Europe

100 TIPS FOR

Traveling with Kids in Europe

E. Ashley Steel & Bill Richards

Rumble Books
Bellevue, Washington

FAMILY ON THE LOOSE: THE ART OF TRAVELING WITH KIDS

First Edition: June 2016

Library of Congress Control Number (LCCN) 2016904648

ISBN 978-0692473870

Published by Rumble Books
Bellevue, Washington 98007
info@rumblebooks.com

Printed in the United States of America

For our kids, Zoey and Logan,
with thanks for all they
have taught us on our family
adventures in Europe.

Contents

Foreword

International family travel is the ultimate adventure and there is no better place than Europe to begin. Your family can explore famous museums and silly waterparks all in the same day. There's delicious food to eat, incredible outdoor landscapes to discover, and plenty of amazing architecture, both old and new, to enjoy. Worried about whether your kids will have fun? Have no fear, ice cream cones can be acquired pretty much everywhere! But seriously, if you are prepared and in good spirits, your kids are likely to have a fantastic experience too. Our hope is to spark new ideas that make your trip successful and fun for everyone. Whatever your goals, our tips can help you be a little more prepared, add a few special experiences to your itinerary, and engage your kids in the planning from beginning to end.

Many folks worry that their kids are not old enough for a big European adventure, or that they won't remember their travel experiences when they get older. Kids are never too young to travel! We start reading to our kids long before we expect them to remember or even understand the story. Why? Because it's fun, gives us a great way to interact and engage with them, and fosters a life-long love of learning. For the same reasons, it's never too early to start exploring the world with your kids. There is no age limit on the joys of riding on a train, exploring a cobblestone alley, or staring at a giant painting. As parents, you can enjoy and even learn from your children's reactions to new places and new people. Their smiles will invite strangers to interact and their attempts at foreign language will encourage comradery and new friendships. Travel fosters a life-long passion for cultural exploration, an understanding of the many beautiful ways people can differ, and a commitment to thinking beyond one's own backyard.

Why Europe? Europe offers incredible breadth and diversity, but the distance between destinations is often quite small. In a few hours, you can travel through multiple languages, diets, and histories. Most Europeans speak two, three, or even four languages, but you can get by with only English. Although there are enough famous landmarks to fill a bookstore with guidebooks, there are even more small towns worthy of lingering visits. You can explore the very old and beautiful as well as the very modern and stunning. And although European children do lots of the same "kid things" as other children, they don't always do them in the same way. Make sure you visit a children's museum, swimming pool, and playground just to see how different these pastimes can be! This book has tips to get you and your family thinking and planning for all of these adventures.

On our first family trip to Europe, we sported diaper bags, carried a stroller wherever we went, and always had a plan for on-the-go naptimes. Although our kids are teenagers now and we've returned many times for new adventures over the years, we still enjoy planning our trips together and discovering new places as a family. Our experience with traveling as a family laid the groundwork for our first book, *Family on the Loose: The Art of Traveling with Kids,* where we offered advice and information for how to travel with children rather than on where to take a family trip. This book focuses only on Europe, blends ideas for how to travel with specific kid-friendly destinations, and is intended to be a quick read for busy parents. Most of these tips originate from personal experience, but we have also included a few tips suggested to us by other traveling families, as well as recommendations for some destinations we long to visit.

Our tips are organized into three sections. The first, "Ready, Set . . . ," will help you prepare for your trip. It provides ideas for involving the kids in planning, packing, and setting an itinerary. Where should we go? What should we bring? And, what should the kids do to get ready? The second section, "Go!," is all about the trip itself—from the plane ride to the hotel room to daily adventures. In addition to safety tips and logistics, you'll find scores of ideas for places to go and things to do. Is Europe a good place for volcanoes? Actually, yes! How many kinds of boat trips can you pack into a three-week vacation? A lot! Can you bring a toddler to a museum? Absolutely! While we can't list all of the tourist activities across this exciting continent, we try to sow the seeds for what your trip can really be. Don't settle for just the Eiffel Tower, the Colosseum, and Big Ben. Explore Europe! Find a sculpture of a ballet dancer in an art museum, eat seven kinds of waffles, go punting, and see the sewers.

The final section, "Home Again," has a great selection of tips for making memories stick, staying connected with the cultures you visited, and sharing your experiences with friends at home. It's all too easy for a vacation to simply slip away into the chaos of returning to "normal." But isn't the goal to come home to a slightly new normal? Of course, the 100th tip may be the most important as it captures our philosophy of family travel. Now that our kids are teenagers, we all look back on our travel adventures as some of the most important family time we've shared.

A Note on the Photographs in This Book

The photographs in this book were all taken by young tourists. We are grateful to the many families and photographers who shared their work, providing our readers with artistic insight into Europe as seen through the eyes of children. You'll be surprised at some of the amazing angles and contrasts provided by our teenage photographers and amused at the variety of details captured by our youngest photographers. Flip through the photos without even reading any tips for visual advice on how to focus your family adventure.

PART 1

READY, SET. . .

Get ready for a fun, entertaining, educational, and sometimes challenging journey! This first section begins with tips for getting you and your kids engaged and excited. The more creativity and care you bring to planning your trip, the better your outcome will be. We also provide lots of ideas to help you pack successfully, book transportation and lodging, and save money in the process.

Preparing for
Adventure

Create a Kid-Designed Journey

TIP
1

Y ou want this trip to belong to everyone in the family. You yearn for the kids to be excited, engaged, and enthusiastic while you're on the road and you hope to build wonderful memories of a trip well taken. How do you make that happen? Include the kids in the planning process!

Start by asking them what they want to see or do. Give them choices. With a three-year-old, for instance, you could flip through a kid's nonfiction book about one of your destinations and let them choose what they might want to visit — say a particular statue. Make a photocopy of "their statue" to bring along on the trip. Now they have a goal and a little control over the family's itinerary.

As kids get older, they can help with internet research and bigger picture decisions. There are so many possible decision points. Stay in an apartment or a hotel? Add a day for an eccentric museum or a scenic train ride? Spend an extra day in Pisa or Florence? Give them a budget, a time frame, and some logistical parameters, then set them free to contribute to your family itinerary. With some confidence, the kids could then take turns being in charge of planning the activities for one day or for one destination. They could also be responsible for researching the history of a particular place that you plan to visit and then educating the rest of the family. Whatever they come up with is a win-win

Carcassonne, France by Sam J., Age 10

situation — you receive travel planning assistance and they become invested in making the trip a success.

Visit Your Local Library

Preparing your kids for an overseas trip can seem daunting. You want them to know a little about history, culture, and language. You want them to be excited and ready to explore. But how will you help them learn to say "thank you" in Finnish or Croatian? No worries, you can find almost everything you need at your local library! It's one stop and it's all free: destination-specific kid's books (both fiction and nonfiction), language tapes, books on CD, slightly out-of-date travel guides, movies, documentaries, cultural craft books, and cookbooks from all over the world. The more kids know about your destination, the more excited they will be when they arrive. With younger kids, try making a craft they might encounter on the trip. Or try making regional food at home, such as paella or crepes, so they will want to taste the real thing on-location. Kids can learn an amazing deal about customs, famous places, art, and historical context simply by browsing a few nonfiction children's books. In fact, parents usually learn a good amount too. If your kids resist the idea of reading and preparing for themselves, have them dig up facts to tell you later at the dinner table, or dare them to prepare a test on destination facts for you. They'll learn as they prepare the test questions and enjoy the opportunity to be the one in charge of handing out grades.

TIP 2

Encourage Teenage Know-It-Alls

TIP

3

elping to build enthusiasm for travel in younger kids is one thing, but what about the all-too-cool teenager? Teens will also be better travelers with a little background knowledge, but they might not be completely on-board with your educational efforts. Start by making a deal! For example, you could increase their limited screen time, but only for movies that have something to do with your travel destination. Perhaps a movie set during the Renaissance or during World War I, or a current foreign-language film. In the months leading up to your trip, encourage documentaries, classics, and independent European films (there are many on Netflix). They'll soon discover that it's more fun to visit a place when you have a little insight in advance. After the films, nudge them toward researching topics they found interesting or that you know might engage them *en route*. For example, ask them to find out everything they can about the *Magna Carta* and share it with you or with their siblings. Or they could put together a collection of maps of Europe at different times, figure out who the Hapsburgs were and how they managed to gain so much power, or find a dozen ways that ancient Greek society still influences modern day life. Their internet research, YouTube discoveries, unusual movie selections, and fun facts are likely to enrich the whole family's trip.

Barcelona, Spain by Ben, Age 14

Paper Maps Rock

There are some amazing tools for exploring the geography of the world, including your family's European destinations. Traditional globes and atlases put the world in perspective. Google Earth allows you to simulate the flight from home to anywhere on the planet, map your route, find a hotel at a convenient location, and sometimes even see playground equipment in neighborhood parks. There are smart phone apps and countless websites. But there is nothing better than a big paper map!

TIP 4

A paper map allows you and the kids to view and touch the whole travel landscape at once, to see the possibilities, and to plan, draw, and re-draw your proposed route. Take it with you to help find your way. You might want a big map of all of Europe so you can highlight your entire route as you go. Or you might want a map for each country, to get a closer perspective on local details. Lay the map out on the floor as you plan. Point out all the amazing information that you can read off of a map — place names, topography, cardinal directions, time zones, the proximity of the closest swimming lake to your hotel. Use it to find off-the-beaten-path opportunities, figure out where the mountains and rivers are located, or put country borders in context. Hang the map on the wall as you plan and stick pins where you book lodging. The map can also be a great vehicle for getting travel advice from friends. Whenever anyone visits your house, ask them to point out where they've been and what they recommend.

Granada, Spain by Gavin, Age 13

Parlez, Hablo, Sprechen

Wherever you are heading in Europe, you can expose your kids to the language(s) they'll hear before you leave home. Empower them to learn a few phrases in each language in advance. It is so much more fun to greet people in their native language, and the reception your kids' efforts receive will likely make it all worthwhile. There is no need for fluency; just a few words can make all the difference in being polite or even, more selfishly, in getting something that they want. It's a great lesson for your kids that, even though English is everywhere in the tourist world, the tourist also bears language responsibility.

Absolute basics include:
* *Hello, goodbye*
* *Please, thank you*
* *I would like . . .* (you can point after that)
* *1, 2, 3, 4, 5, 6, 7, 8, 9, 10, 20, 30 . . . 100*
* *Excuse me / I'm sorry / You're welcome*

A few other phrases that are often very handy:
* *Delicious!*
* *Where is the bathroom?*
* *Do you speak English?*
* *Is this okay?* (Useful in an amazing number of situations)

Easy language-learning possibilities can be found in the bookstore, library, school, or ethnic restaurant. Authentic ethnic restaurants are a particularly fun language exposure option! You get to eat as you learn and, for intermediate-level language learners, have the opportunity to practice the all-important basics of ordering in a restaurant. There are also an impressive number of internet options including websites dedicated to language learning, online language exchanges, and kid's television programming in foreign languages. You might download podcasts that enable your kids to learn languages in the car or while waiting for siblings to finish activities. Of course, regular old language cassettes, CDs, and DVDs still do the trick. Recordings that include songs are particularly helpful with kids. Language learning videos full of songs and music are available from many vendors but they tend to be expensive. Most public libraries have a wide variety of options to loan. Some libraries even rent language-learning software or can provide access to online language-learning through the library website.

Time for a Timeline

TIP 6

When America was born, people in Europe had already been playing and listening to Johann Sebastian Bach's music for over 50 years. Construction of the Notre Dame cathedral in Paris started 837 years before the turn of the last century and took 182 years to finish in 1345. So the construction phase on that one building lasted almost as long as the United States has been around. And then there's the really old stuff like the Colosseum and Stonehenge. As an adult, it's truly mind-boggling to keep perspective on human history while traveling through Europe. To young kids, for whom last year was a very long time ago, or to teens, who call songs from 2010 "oldies," the task can seem impossible.

A little timeline carefully catalogued onto a roll of blank receipt paper can help put things in perspective. Better yet, use a big strip of butcher paper to make an impressively large timeline that runs all the way down your hallway. Start with easy dates in your family's history, such as birth dates and wedding anniversaries. Then dig a little deeper to include the year your house was built or when your state achieved statehood. What's the oldest building in your town? Paste a picture of it on your timeline. Next, add the dates associated with places you plan to visit on your trip. What is the oldest landmark on your itinerary? If your timeline is small enough, take it with you on your trip to add important dates as you go. Can you figure out how old the hotels are that you'll be staying in? You might sleep in a room that's older than your state!

Athens, Greece by Jeffrey, Age 10

Shoes Matter

E uropeans walk a lot! It's a good bet that, when in Europe, your kids will walk a lot too. Whether you expect your "waddler" to push the stroller at times, your four-year-old to enjoy a traipse through Bruges, or your teenager to manage several days of hiking the *Camino de Santiago* in northern Spain, you'll all need to have the right equipment. Everyone in the family needs to have at least one good pair of walking shoes. This pair of shoes doesn't have heels or slippery soles, and it does have support. And it most definitely is not flip-flops. These other shoes have their place, but it's not walking all day on uneven terrain. Choose practical shoes that are sturdy, maybe even have arch supports, and that can weather a rainstorm. Help your

TIP

7

Rome, Italy by Geneva, Age 13

kids select a pair of shoes that are unlikely to blister, that can be worn in the heat, and can withstand long-distance mileage. If in doubt, ask at the shoe store or try specialty shoe stores designed for walking, travel, and outdoor activities.

Walk, Walk, Walk

Like everything else, walking well takes practice, and you'll want your family in good walking shape. Take some leisurely strolls around the neighborhood, try walking to school, plan a few short hikes, or take an all-day excursion into your own city. If you practice walking before the trip you'll get in shape, avoid blisters (have Band-Aids handy anyway, just in case), and possibly head off temper fits on the road. Prior to setting out, help the kids understand how far they are expected to walk, how often they might get carried or sit in the stroller, and what they will be expected to carry. Praise them for a job well done; count steps if you have to; set reasonable goals; and don't let fussing lead to a piggy-back ride. If they really need a break, have them reach an attainable goal first: "If you walk two more blocks, you can get back in the stroller." Once you've set those walking expectations, keep it fun. Even practice walks need rest stops and ice cream cones.

TIP 8

Managing Logistics

Label Your Kids

O kay, maybe you can't literally "label your kids," but it is a great idea to bejewel them with emergency contact information. If, by chance, one of your children were to get lost *en route*, you want to make a reunion quick and easy. For the youngest kids, there are ID bracelets. These can be purchased from vendors that sell medical alert bracelets. It might be best to leave the child's name off the bracelet and, instead, save the space for your cell phone number (if it works in Europe), your hotel phone numbers (if you have just a few), and a relative somewhere who can be counted on for help in a crisis. If you plan to have lots of stops, it might even be worth investing in a couple of bracelets so that your child always has a local phone number on their wrist. Note that you will probably need to order the ID bracelets a few weeks in advance of your trip. Engraved pet tags might work in a pinch. You can have them made in minutes at machines found in most pet stores, although they don't hold nearly as much information.

Older kids might be trusted with a necklace, charm bracelet, or key chain that contains a small slip of paper with all the important contact information. Again, check pet stores. You may be able to find tiny hollow barrels meant for temporary pet identification. You can also tape the information inside a favorite baseball cap or on a luggage tag that floats inside

Chianti, Italy by Finn, Age 9

each child's backpack. If kids are old enough to carry a wallet or travel money belt, slip in a sheet of paper with a photocopy of their passport information on one side and your itinerary with addresses, dates, and phone numbers on the other.

Pack Even Lighter

Everyone says to "pack light," but you should try to one-up them and pack even lighter! Traveling successfully, especially with small children, means having the essentials on hand without being overwhelmed by heavy, bulky bags. Although it's tempting to pack for every possibility, especially on your first overseas trip, resist this urge and remember that there are kids in Europe too. They sell Band-Aids, toys, and spare clothes in every single European country. All you really, really need are your personal medical essentials and a sense of humor. Think through the items you are truly likely to need and be creative about how to stay light and still have it all. For example, in your carry-on or day bag, you'll want one change of clothes for each infant and toddler. Pack the outfit in a zip-top bag and suck all the air out. Tuck it at the very bottom of your bag. The plastic-wrapped spare clothes provide a moisture barrier in case you set your bag down in spilled coffee or on a wet park bench. The zip-top bag also comes in handy if there is a big spill or an accident, in which case you can use it to keep the messy clothes contained. Compressible rain jackets are worth their weight in gold.

TIP 10

Paris, France by Jordan, Age 10

Pack extra-light in the toy department and be creative instead — seemingly humdrum travel items like plastic spoons or empty cups can entertain infants and small children. A simple deck of cards can provide hours of solo and family entertainment for older kids.

Wean yourself off your own weighty wardrobe. You likely won't be meeting people more than once or twice so you really don't need lots of different outfits. Be prepared to wash clothes and let them drip dry overnight in hotel rooms. This might sound like a hassle but dragging heavy bags down a cobblestone street is so much more of a burden. Remember to save a little room in your luggage for new purchases. One way to make extra room in your suitcase for coming home is to give some of your clothes away *en route*. For example, before you leave home, buy a few cheap t-shirts for the kids that you will be more than ready to donate after several sweaty weeks of travel.

Compartmentalize the Packing

Packing efficiently can be the secret to traveling light and fast. Once you've boiled your packing list down to the essentials, organize everything into small bags. Packing cubes can be found at most outdoor or travel stores. While pricey, they really do help you stay organized on the road. Give one cube to each kid and have them squeeze their own clothes inside. Or, use one cube to keep a dressy outfit for each family member tucked out of the way when not needed. Resealable plastic bags can serve a similar purpose. Freezer bags usually have a patch for labeling with a permanent marker. Each child might keep all of his socks and underwear in one bag or be allowed one bag for small toys and games. Don't forget a trash bag for compartmentalizing the stinky laundry.

TIP 11

Emporiatrics

The medical specialty dedicated to the health problems of world travelers is called emporiatrics. Most of us will need few, if any, shots for visiting Europe but it's a good idea to talk to a travel doctor well in advance of any trip. They likely have access to Travax, an in-depth and constantly updated travel information website specifically for health professionals. Colleges and universities often have terrific travel clinics. You can get a lot of information yourself through the U.S. government's Centers for Disease Control and Prevention (CDC) travel website, but note that they are U.S.-centric. For example, there is no mention of European tick-borne encephalitis (TBE), perhaps because there is no vaccine available in the U.S. Check the European Centre for Disease Prevention and Control (ECDC) website for specific information about the countries where you plan to travel.

TIP 12

Health clinics will need a copy of your immunization records and a general itinerary for your trip. They will wonder if you plan to be in rural areas, the backcountry, or staying on farms. Even though you probably won't need anything special for a trip to Europe, the doctor or nurse at the travel clinic will help you get your family's immunizations up-to-date (a nice pre-travel precaution) and will probably talk to your children about basics such as washing hands, being careful crossing the street,

Normandy, France by LJ, Age 4

using car seats and seat belts, and even using life-jackets or helmets. It's nice to have a professional remind your kids, especially teens who may be, just maybe, less likely to listen to you.

The First-Aid Kit

A small first-aid kit is essential for any trip. It should have medications as well as basic first-aid supplies. Medications include everything you might need for common illnesses, discomforts, or injuries. Infant and child acetaminophen and ibuprofen can be difficult to find in some European countries so are absolutely worth carrying with you. And adult over-the-counter medications that you commonly take, especially anything containing pseudoephedrine, is probably easier to carry along than to try and find in-country. First-aid supplies should be sufficient to manage bumps and scrapes not requiring a visit to the doctor.

There are many ways to shrink the weight and volume of your first-aid kit without sacrificing completeness. First, consider whether you really need a large quantity of each item or just a small supply. Many over-the-counter medications can be purchased (though often for an exaggerated cost) in single dose packaging. Check local drugstore chains and travel/outdoor stores. Prepackaged first-aid kits can be a great source of these convenient items, even if you do not use everything in the kit (you can always put unused items in the back of your car).

TIP 13

You can take most medications out of their cardboard packaging but be careful to keep all medications labeled and retain instructions for their use (either a side of the box or an insert). Tape instructions to the bottle or to the sheet of pills and pack them together in a small plastic baggie. Check with your family doctor for prescription medications, such as antibiotics, to be used in emergencies. If your children aren't old enough to swallow pills, you may request liquid antibiotics in powder-form — just add water on the road if necessary. Of course, make sure your kids do not have ready access to your first-aid kit full of prescription and over-the-counter drugs, many of which look invitingly like candy. Consider carrying your medications in a nontransparent cosmetic bag, fixed with a small luggage lock.

Baby Basics

The equipment for traveling with babies and toddlers can feel overwhelming. Consider a few small-size essentials that allow you to pack light even with a tiny traveler. All are inexpensive and relatively easy to find. A portable changing station is an absolute must! You don't really want to lug around a big diaper bag and you definitely don't want to lie your baby down on random floors and changing tables all over Europe. A portable changing station is just a roll-up changing pad with some pockets for diapers, wipes, and plastic baggies. Tuck it right into your day pack. Sippy cup tops that fit on regular cups and even on water bottles can save you from spills, stains, and endlessly washing a big, bulky sippy cup. Baby toy links are a fantastic travel solution. They serve as teethers, toys, and as a way to attach oddities to your backpack. They can also be used to keep other toys from tumbling onto dirty train and restaurant floors. Lastly, "travel high chairs" are fantastic. They aren't really high chairs at all but a compact, cloth system for securing a baby to a regular dining chair.

TIP 14

Strollers

Here's the catch with strollers: while there are all kinds of really cool, sturdy, and expensive models on the market, these aren't always easy or efficient to fold up and carry on an airplane, bus, or subway. Of course they're made for kid comfort and ease of maneuvering, but maybe not for ease of travel. On the flip side, there are very lightweight umbrella strollers that are easy to transport, but maybe aren't so comfortable or rugged for the pedestrian streets of old European cities. If you need to bring a stroller to preserve the tiny legs in your family, or provide a place for little-kid down time on the road, which is best? It really depends on your preferences and child's mobility. With the youngest kids that are likely to spend a large part of each travel day in a stroller, you'll probably want to prioritize sturdiness and comfort over ease of jumping on a train. As kids get a little more mobile and you need the stroller for shorter periods of each day, maybe you can get away with a cheapo lightweight model. An umbrella stroller may get trashed after a few weeks on the cobblestone streets, but with a little duct tape or wire from hangers found in hotel closets, it could last the entire trip, providing convenient relief when needed.

TIP 15

County Galway, Ireland by Caelan, Age 7

Money Matters

Budgets may be dreary subjects but they are a reality for most travelers and, by extension, a reality for most traveling kids. Talk about this early on and get the kids involved. What's a realistic daily budget? What sort of trade-offs will you need to make?

TIP 16

As in all aspects of the trip, give the kids a say. Would they prefer to stay in average accommodations every night or do they want to stay in a few super cheap and probably imperfect places in exchange for a special night or activity? Talk a bit in advance with yourself and your family about what financial limits there will be. Can you afford to eat out at a restaurant every meal or will most breakfasts, lunches, and some dinners be picnic affairs? What kinds of inexpensive activities will you all enjoy and learn from while traveling?

Kids generally like to buy stuff, so give them a budget for that too. Perhaps a small amount each day or a small amount at each destination for a souvenir or a special snack. Set clear expectations. For very young kids, the expectation might be "one small souvenir per location and no begging." For teens, the expectation might be as simple as "stay within your budget." The less your kids are tugging on your sleeve at every knickknack vendor, the happier you all will be.

Don't Leave Home Without It

TIP 17

Without what? Money! You don't need to bring a lot of cash with you, but a little safety cash can save the day. Keep some dollars and/or Euros in your wallet, of course, and also hide a little in your daypack and tuck a little more into your

suitcase lining. Things happen. Banks close for holidays you've never heard of, wallets get stolen, cab drivers demand cash, deposits are required, luggage gets locked away overnight, and credit cards can suddenly get declined in the name of fraud protection. If you feel anxious, you can also carry traveler's checks with you but, almost always, a little cash will do the trick.

Ola, Santorini, Greece by Geneva, Age 13

Call Ahead!

TIP 18

Fraud prevention at most credit card companies is working hard to save you from thieves who might steal your credit card number and flee to a foreign country. When you and your family are the ones fleeing to a foreign country, this can be a problem. After one or two purchases, you may find that your credit card gets denied. If this happens, you simply need to call the company and provide enough identifying information, often including a list of recent purchases, to convince them of your identity. They can then remotely unlock the card; however, finding a phone or postponing a purchase can be a big hassle. For example, no one wants to be trying to buy train tickets just a few minutes before departure and suddenly have their credit card frozen. To prevent fraud prevention from wreaking havoc, simply call the credit card company before you leave home to register your travel plans. Use the 800 number on the back of your card about a week in advance of your trip and provide your full itinerary. If family members will be in two different countries simultaneously at any point during your trip, be sure to let them know that.

For example, if one adult arrives in Europe a few days in advance of the rest of the family's arrival, credit card charges may start accruing in both Europe and your home country on the same day. Such double-location billing is extremely likely to trigger your credit card company's fraud prevention department if you don't warn them in advance.

Prepare to Spend Wisely

Most travelers use a combination of credit cards and ATM/debit cards. Both of these types of cards usually offer the interbank exchange rate, saving you money as compared to traveler's checks or converting foreign currency yourself. But beware of fees! While you are on the phone telling your bank about your travel itinerary, ask them about their currency conversion fees, foreign transaction fees, and foreign ATM fees. These can add up. Plan to make as few electronic transactions as possible and minimize foreign currency exchanges once you're on the road. For example, you might plan to put big purchases on the credit card and maximize the amount of cash withdrawn from ATMs with each transaction (while withdrawing no more local currency than what you will actually need in-country).

TIP 19

It could be worth applying for a new credit card. Chip and PIN technology is prevalent across Europe. You may find that you need a credit or ATM card with a chip in order to use kiosks, pump gas, or even pay your restaurant bill. If your credit card doesn't already have a security chip, try requesting one from your bank. If they aren't available through your bank, consider applying for a new card. Also note that a few banks offer credit cards with no foreign transaction fees at all. If you have a long trip planned, it may be worth applying for one of these. *(Tip idea inspired by Caroline Goodner.)*

Planning Your Itinerary

Embrace the Adventure

To enhance the sense of adventure in your family travels, don't have all of your plans set in stone. Keep some of your options open so that you can change your mind midstream. Sure, having your first and last couple of nights' lodging booked will give you peace of mind and prevent disaster. But in the middle of your trip, after you have observed the lay of the land, it might be fun to play it by ear for a few nights, to go where interest takes you and opportunity beckons. Try arriving in a new town and choosing a hotel based on how it looks in real life rather than how it was rated on the internet. Spontaneity might bring you something unique rather than more of the same.

TIP 20

This philosophy also applies to the daily scale of travel life. Don't schedule your whole day with activities. Leave parts of most days for doing whatever you discover along the way. There are bound to be cool things right around the corner that you could never plan for ahead of time. Walk down the street looking for a place to eat while you still have time to discover a playground or stumble on an artist gallery.

Pisa, Italy by Alexa, Age 13

Budget Airline Flights for Pennies

Budget airlines fly all over Europe and frequently have prices that are amazingly low, sometimes even less than a dollar before tax! These airlines are generally not covered by larger search engines and frequently do not have flights servicing major airports. To discover companies with flights that might suit your family's itinerary, try searching Wikipedia for "discount airlines" or "low-cost airlines." There will be an extensive list of small airlines organized by country. Pay special attention to exactly which airport you'll fly in and out of, guarantees (or lack thereof) in case of flight delays or cancellation, and extra fees. In some cases, you have to pay extra for traveling without a European passport, pay extra to talk to a live person on the phone, or pay extra for a guaranteed seat. Remember though, most flights are pretty quick so the discomfort or frustration is likely to be short-lived.

TIP 21

By choosing discount airlines, you may discover fabulous new cities you hadn't planned on visiting. Ryanair, for example, flies into Bratislava instead of Vienna and Girona instead of Barcelona. You could hop on a one-hour bus shuttle into the bigger city. But Bratislava and Girona are fabulous places with trendy restaurants and cobblestone streets. Why rush off? Similarly, Transavia flies out of Eindhoven, The Netherlands. Sure, you don't want to miss Amsterdam, but Einhoven has the Centrum Kunstlicht in de Kunst (Artificial Light in Art Centre) right next door to the fascinating Philips Museum that was once a light bulb factory. You can shed new light on Van Gogh, so to speak.

But keep in mind, since airline delays are common and transfers to major cities are generally required, low-cost airlines aren't the best option on a tight schedule or just before a major deadline, such as a work meeting or a cruise ship departure.

Overnight Trains Are So Cool!

TIP 22

Made classic by so many films through the years, is there anything more European than sleeping on a train? Picture walking through an old city to the train station, locating the correct platform, waiting for your train to arrive, finding the right berth in your sleeper car, and spending the night chugging overland to a new place. Most kids (and adults) are pretty enthralled by the idea of sleeping on a train, by the chairs that convert to beds, by the little sink in the corner, and by the train sounds and rocking motion that make falling asleep both easier and harder. And don't forget about the dining car and the creepy toilet down the hall. It's all part of the thrill.

Though overnight trains can be significantly more expensive than planes, you save the expense of a hotel room for the night. And there's the simplicity of not having to worry about airport shuttles, lines, and security. If you really want to maximize your transportation cool-factor, book a train from Germany to Sweden. Your train will travel onboard a ferry across the Baltic Sea and your kids can boast that they rode on a train on a boat!

During peak holiday times, booking train tickets

Porto, Portugal by LJ, Age 5

and reserving a sleeping cabin, couchette (bed), or even reclining seat should be done online well in advance. During the off-season or if you're flexible, you can generally walk up to a ticket counter, purchase a ticket, and make a reservation for a place to sleep on the next train. Private cabins are generally the most expensive, but come with their own sink and the flexibility to go to bed and wake up on your own schedule. Couchettes are usually six sleeping berths per cabin and are reserved one by one, so unless you have a big family you should expect to share the cabin. This means converting from a seat to a bed (and vice versa) at the same time as everyone else, and using the sink in the bathroom down the hall to brush your teeth. Note that train tickets and reservations are two separate items — with just a train ticket, you and your kiddos could end up standing up from Oslo to Rome.

Go Off-Season

A great way to see popular sights with shorter or nonexistent lines, and maybe even at a discount, is to go when others don't. In the winter, head to the Louvre, Big Ben, or the Colosseum in relative peace. You may not be able to eat at the outdoor café, but getting to see the Mona Lisa or David will be whole lot easier. And it's not just the major attractions that can be more manageable in the down season; you can have your choice of cool rooms at classic hotels on, for example, the Spanish coast if you go when the others stay home. Be careful though, some places, like Venice, are so popular that even the off-season may seem pretty crowded. If you do go to Venice in the off-season, bring rubber boots!

TIP 23

There's No Place Like Home

Consider renting an apartment at least once during your journey. Hotels are easy, B&Bs are fun, but an apartment is most like having a home away from home. There's a living room where you can relax as a group and often a place for parents to sleep behind the privacy of a closed door. Apartments in classic buildings can give you a flavor of what life is like in a country where history goes back more than a few hundred years. Your kids might discover that the toilet isn't in the bathroom or that a small kitchen can be amazingly functional. Grocery shopping in Europe is fun, so try out the kitchen with breakfast or a stay-at-home dinner. And the best thing about apartments is that they can be particularly economical for families.

Apartments are usually easy to find by searching online. Often there is an association of apartment owners, even in small cities, that coordinate an internet presence. In other cities, one company will control many apartment options. Check-in is usually at a rental office where you get a key and directions to the apartment. Occasionally, you'll meet the owner at the apartment itself. Rental companies and owners may be able to watch your bags before check-in or after check-out.

The reservation process will likely require you to exchange a few e-mails to get all the details organized, and there is often a minimum stay. Apartments are best for locations where you're planning to stay at least a few days. Be careful to choose

Burano, Italy by Alexa, Age 13

an apartment in the best location for your family, either close to the attractions or someplace quieter.

If you're planning a stay of a week or more, another option to consider is a home exchange. Home exchanges take a little more logistical work up front but can be a fun and economical opportunity. As with any lodging, don't take for granted that the balcony is childproof, the hot water won't scald, or that the electrical outlets are protected.

Glamp It Up!

TIP 25

Consider camping. Wait, wait, not that rustic American tent experience. Europe does holiday camps that are difficult to describe. Giant waterslides and treehouses, golf courses and indoor spas. There can be shops, organized tours, Turkish baths, fresh bread delivery . . . some even rent duvets! Just search "European holiday camps," show your kids the photos, and ask if they want to go.

Icons Are Icons

TIP 26

Kids like to brag to their friends, even about trips. And a trip to Europe typically involves visiting at least a few of the sites that everyone has heard of, like Big Ben, the Eiffel Tower, the leaning tower of Pisa, the Little Mermaid. As much as well-traveled parents may want to avoid such icons and the challenges of squeezing into an already crowded tourist center, kids may be particularly excited for these same spots. They want bragging rights for the "must-see" places and to be able to compare stories with other kids back home.

Icons are awesome places to look *at* another culture, but since they're usually packed with everyone but locals, they aren't terribly good places to look *into* another culture. As you set up your itinerary, strike a balance between the quintessential

Paris, France photo and filters by Alexa, Age 13

travel destinations that you will share with throngs of tourists from around the world, and small, truly local European experiences.

Leave Something out

TIP
27

A lot of pressure can come with a big trip: planning the perfect itinerary, being able to afford it, hoping the kids enjoy it as much as you dream that they will, seeing all the once-in-a-lifetime sites. A way to help relieve some of this pressure is to leave something out of your itinerary. You don't have to do and see everything just because you are finally making the epic trip to Europe. First of all, it's just too big, diverse, and interesting. You won't be able to make much of a dent in European culture on one visit. The Louvre by itself is hard to cover in one visit (impossible with kids), let alone all of Paris. Go at your own family pace and try not to feel like you are missing out. You never know what opportunities might be afforded to you and your kids in the future. You will probably be back on a work trip, another family trip, or a second honeymoon after the kids go to college. Your kids will likely be back as exchange or study-abroad students, on a summer backpacking adventure, or even on their own honeymoon. You want this trip to whet the kids' appetite for travel and not entrench the feeling of "been there, done that." Always leave something to do the next time you come back.

PART 2

GO!

In this next section, we're offering up tips for being en voyage, as they say. First, we share pointers to help you enjoy the plane flight and airport, as well as the basics of daily life away from home. Then we'll delve into offbeat destinations and kid-centric travel themes. You may want to skim these ideas in advance to help design an exciting itinerary. Other tips in this section will help you keep everyone safe, happy, engaged, and well-fed while you're traveling. You'll even find ideas for making a visit to an art museum fun and exciting!

Taking Flight

Carry-on Independence

TIP 28

Parents can't be responsible for all of the family's stuff on the plane. Everyone is a traveler; everyone should have their own carry-on bag. The youngest kids might only carry a few things in a tiny pack — for example, plane presents or little bags of snacks — but anything they can put in their backpack is one less thing in yours. Plus, being in charge of their own backpack is a good start to being a responsible traveler. As kids get older, you can expect them to pack their own carry-on, and they can also help with common items like cameras, portable computers, and bigger snacks. A personal pack provides independence and a surprising amount of learning as kids choose what goes in and what doesn't. They discover what they really need to have on-board, what they regret lugging around, and what happens when something is forgotten or lost.

Tag Teddy

TIP 29

It's a very sad day when a teddy bear or blankie gets left onboard a plane or train and is lost forever. They slip between the seats when kids are sleeping, get tucked into unexpected places, or get missed during the hubbub of gathering adult valuables and cranky kids at the end of a long journey. It's a tragedy you'll want to avoid. You can help prevent disaster by putting an identification tag on your favorite stuffy just like any other travel item. You might even use personalized labels designed to keep kid's clothes from getting lost at camp or school. These labels also work well for travel clothes,

Ring of Kerry, Ireland by Lillie, Age 8

kid packs, and sneakers. Make sure to include your e-mail address. Why? Because e-mail is free and will reach you wherever you are. You will also want to grab a luggage tag at check-in and attach it to the bear, rabbit, or blanket corner. If it doesn't attach naturally, use a safety pin. The tag will get folks' attention! When you fill out the tag, write "Best Friend — Please Return" or some other note that will tug at the heart of even the grumpiest maintenance staff, plus detailed contact information for the next week. Hopefully, if teddy runs into trouble, you will all be quickly reunited.

Active Airport Games

You're supposed to get to the airport way ahead of departure time for international flights, which often leaves you with an hour or two to kill once you've jumped the ticketing and security hurdles. And if you have to switch planes, there is likely to be even more extended terminal time. Take advantage of this lull in your schedule and the expanse of the airport to help burn off kids' energy before confining them in a plane. Active games are a fun way to tame your kids' excitement prior to the flight.

TIP 30

Try our airport obstacle course. It's simple: Give instructions for kids to follow that build memory and release energy. Perhaps start with something easy like "walk over to that pillar, go around it three times, and skip back." You can get progressively more complicated and include jumping jacks, sit-ups, circles around trash cans, tracing patterns on the floor, sprints, hops, leaps, and even somersaults. Pick a spot where you won't bother other travelers and remind your kids regularly to be considerate.

Plane Presents Are Awesome

TIP 31

Before everyone, including the tiniest of children, had their own fleet of electronic gadgets to keep themselves amused during a long plane flight, there were plane presents. These were small items collected over time from various sources (for example, impulse buys at the drugstore check-out counter), wrapped in gift paper, and doled out one at a time over the course of a long flight to amuse and entertain. They were cards, puzzles, comic books, crayons, magnets, candy — almost anything to focus attention for a few moments away from the tedium at hand. For very young children, plane presents might have been as simple as a collection of orange juice can lids. As kids aged, plane presents got suitably more sophisticated to include miniature kaleidoscopes, coloring pages, and brain teasers. Sometimes the kids' carry-on backpack was entirely filled with the excitement of little wrapped presents. Even now, in the age of personal screens on every seatback, plane presents can still be an effective, entertaining, and creative diversion. Try it out!

Strasbourg, France by Maya, Age 7

Look Out Below!

TIP 32

Pictures of Earth from space are always impressive. We gain perspective, learn geology, see our own hometown in a new way, and maybe even pick up a little geography. The view from your plane is almost as good. Spend some time looking out the window with your kids. Daytime and nighttime both work, but cloudy days are not the most interesting. Bring a paper map and try to pick out your flight path. Try to find key landmarks and help your kids orient themselves from the air. Rivers can be particularly helpful for figuring out which way is which.

Explore the terrain. Where are all the urban centers located and why? What does the road network look like? What's different between countries? At night, take a look at how many lights you can see. How are they distributed? Where are the darkest areas and why? Try creating a scavenger hunt or bingo card for items that can be found looking out of the window. Things to include might be highways, lakes, sports fields, farm fields, factories, airports, and maybe castles. Note: If you want to take pictures from the air, turn your cell phone to airplane mode before you shut it down at take off, then you can turn it on during the flight to use as a camera.

Schwangau, Germany by Ilsa, Age 13

Living on the Loose

The Daypack

Every family needs one, or maybe two, vessels to carry the day's supplies. All day, every day, you'll need to help your kids behave well, have fun, and stay safe as you navigate and enjoy a new place. Your daypack is the toolbox with which you can ensure such travel happiness: raingear, sunscreen, hats, snacks, first aid, guidebooks, phones. You may also want to throw in books, crayons, journals, and a deck of cards to help you get through the waiting times. If you have little ones, you'll want to have diaper essentials and a spare change of clothes squeezed into a plastic bag with you at all times. Exactly what stuff you need will depend on your kids, the weather, and your location. You want to bring enough stuff to stay happy and safe, but not so much that it slows you down or hurts your back.

What should you look for in a daypack? It should be big enough to carry the basics your family needs but no bigger. You'll also appreciate an easy-access pocket for snacks and other non-valuables. If you choose a backpack, make sure it's designed to lie flat against your back even when loaded. Bulky backpacks tend to bang into other people and get stuck in bus doors. Bags that are expandable work very well if you need to carry around a few jackets for part of the day or if you like souvenir shopping.

TIP

33

Zurich, Switzerland by W, Age 2

Manners Matter

TIP 34

When preparing your kids for the trip, discussing cultural respect is essential. Cultural respect is more than simply not offending anyone. You and your family will be representing your home country as you travel, and you don't want to give your own culture or nationality a bad name. Just by being cute and friendly, your kids will buy a lot of goodwill, but a few extra easy ideas include:

* Don't point your finger or camera directly at anybody and always ask before taking someone's picture.
* Speak quietly.
* Keep your feet off of public property such as park benches, train seats, and statues.

* Dress modestly in modest cultures and religious centers.
* Say "Thank You."
* Don't stare.
* Begin with "Excuse me, do you speak English?" in the native language if possible.
* Line up politely in countries where others do the same, and don't get bent out of shape about mob lines in countries where that is the standard operating procedure. You will quickly discover which one is which.

Review in advance any unique aspects of cultural etiquette for each destination.

County Cork, Ireland by Brenna, Age 11

You're Not in Kansas Anymore

Renting a car can be an economical and efficient way to see small towns and big cities alike. Before you go, check the driving laws in every country where you plan to drive. In Slovenia, for example, you are required to drive with your headlights on at all times. Carrying a reflec-

Paris, France by Jessica, Age 13

tive vest, warning triangle, and first-aid kit are also compulsory, and there are steep fines for missing equipment. One wonders how much money the country takes in per year from visitors who aren't aware of these laws.

There's no honking your horn in many major European cities and parking rules can be complicated. Make sure you are insured for any accidents that occur when driving a rental car. Your insurance company at home may cover you when driving abroad. If so, carry proof of insurance. If not, you will want to make sure that you can rely on the rental car company's insurance. Also note that cars with standard transmissions are fairly common. If you want to rent a vehicle with an automatic transmission, you may need to make a special request and pay a bit extra for the convenience.

TIP

35

Safety First!

Europe is a safe place but safety culture is not the same everywhere. In Europe, the responsibility for staying safe lies with the individual. Construction areas, for example, might be wide open and free of signs that say "Warning." It is simply expected that when individuals see large equipment, tripping hazards, and open holes in the ground, they will cross the street and avoid the danger. When we asked our European friends what struck them most about American life, they answered that there was a label on the coffee warning folks that it was hot. In general, they found our ubiquitous warning labels shocking and somewhat comical. Your kids will need to understand that they need to use safety common sense everywhere they go. They also need to know the safety basics: How far away from you are they allowed to wander? How can they find you

TIP 36

or access help if they get lost? Is there anything that's not safe for them to eat? What are the biggest dangers to them? Teach them to watch out for cars and open water. Knowledge, communication, and planning will absolutely help you and your kids stay safe.

Paris, France by Jessica, Age 13

Sleep!

TIP 37

t can be tempting to try to spend every costly travel minute on activities. But good behavior demands sleep and without good behavior those expensive activities won't be very much fun at all. When the kids are little, bring a comfy stroller and plan your day to enable a long, restful nap on wheels. As they get older, you may still want to build in afternoon quiet time. What to do for your teens? Let them sleep in! This may fit right in with your strategy to combat jetlag. Don't sacrifice happy rested kids for the hotel's free breakfast or an early morning excursion. The adults should also sleep when the opportunity presents itself. In other words, sleep when the kids sleep. Just like at home, it won't take long for a sleep deficit to impact temperament — yours or theirs. *(Tip idea inspired by Alicia Patterson.)*

Give the Kids the Camera

t's tempting to photograph your kids everywhere you go. Arrive in a famous place? Line up the kids and say "Say Cheese!" Some kids love this, some tolerate it, and others put up a big, unpleasant stink. Don't forgo all family portraits and iconic kid snaps but shake it up a bit. Nearly all kids like taking photographs themselves. Give them a short-term photo assignment while you wait in line, wait for the bus, or wait for dinner to be served. For example, "find five details that no one usually notices" or "take pictures of three ways you can tell exactly where we are." For younger kids, request a mélange of shoes or statues or leaves. Long-term photo projects can be a trip

TIP 38

highlight. Each child might have their own personal assignment such as "Gargoyles" or "Typical Tourists" or "The Urban/Nature Boundary" or "Transportation." Let them pick their own theme and help them find something challenging. Absolutely do not forget "selfies." Can your tween capture every European landmark and include half her face? A silly face? A model face? In how many places can your teenage son capture his own sneaker?

Interact with Art

TIP 39

Staring at art can be a bit dull, even for parents. Many kids need to participate to really enjoy something. For example, think how much more fun your kids have when visiting a petting zoo versus staring at a wildlife diorama. Interacting with art might include bringing colored pencils and a sketch pad to a museum, taking a series of photos of family members in or on public statues (where it's okay to climb), dressing up a public statue, or being an art critic and writing a review of a museum exhibit in the travel journal. Grumpy kids that are veritably dragged into a museum might particularly enjoy writing a scathing review. They won't realize that they have to observe and think about the exhibit in the process. A fun game is to buy a bunch of postcards of famous paintings and have kids write new titles

Salzburg, Austria by Ricky, Age 7

for them. At the next meal, see if the parents can guess which title goes with which painting or even explain how the new title illuminates a new angle on the artwork. For example, "Lady Who Just Told a Lie" — which painting might that refer to and what would it tell you about the artist's motivation if that really were the title?

Collect Something

I t used to be fun to collect a coin from every country but the adoption of the Euro destroyed that for most of Europe. Old coins are still a possibility if your family enjoys visiting antique shops and second-hand markets. Stamps are still unique in every country, very light, and reasonably cheap. But in the age of electronic correspondence, who goes to the post office anymore? Postcards have become good remembrances. They're cheap, light, particular to each stop along the way, and can add a fun twist to a museum visit. Big museums such as the Louvre or the Victoria and Albert are particularly fun because they have a huge selection of postcards. Young kids love to sort and sift their growing collection and remember the moments of their journey. You might want to purchase duplicate pairs — one to play with, one to save. Consider writing a short note on the back of each postcard describing one particular detail that you want to remember from the day or destination. Other remembrances are completely free. Collect a card from every restaurant, a small rock from every forest trail, coasters, tourist maps, and so on.

TIP 40

Collecting is not a new idea — souvenir stands are everywhere. Kids are drawn to these trinket shops like moths to a flame. Have a plan. For example, you might allow one small souvenir from each city.

It's fun to buy the same item in each place. You might let your kids buy one collectible spoon, miniature doll, statue, magnet, or even a shot glass (for storing earrings, of course) from every city. Definitely decide your plan in advance so you don't need to enter into endless negotiating at every stop. Pre-negotiated price limits are also a wise idea. Those who prefer to keep their kids out of the mass-produced trinket markets might consider supporting local artists by buying one sketch or handmade item from each city. There isn't a major city in Europe without an artist/tourist interface at the edge of a park or outside a popular tourist destination. In smaller cities, you can likely locate shops full of crafts and art from local artisans. Eastern Europe boasts a particularly large collection of artist cooperatives.

Map Souvenirs

Every city provides paper tourist maps and these are a perfect (and generally free!) souvenir. Give the map to a kid and have them navigate your family to the museum, back to the hotel, or just around the town. Use a highlighter to record your daily route (different colors for different days), circle museums visited, or even annotate with sketches and notes. Either paste the maps into your travel journal or save a map from every city in a big envelope. Once at home, you might photograph each highlighted map and insert into a photobook alongside the photos from each destination; punch holes and file the maps in a big three-ring binder; pin the maps up on a giant bulletin board; or place the maps under a glass table top. If your trip is long enough, you could wallpaper a bathroom!

TIP
41

Travel Apps

TIP
42

t would be impossible to list all of the cool travel apps out there. The smartphone world is forever changing and there's no way to stay current. Just know that there is an app for almost everything you might imagine. Enjoy an internet search to discover those that have been developed for tourists and locals in your specific destinations, general travel apps, and kid-entertainment apps. Like all apps, some are free and others are not. When searching for and downloading apps while traveling, be conscious of roaming charges and where to find free Wi-Fi (yes, there is an app for that).

Kid-centric apps focus on entertainment, namely games and videos. These are obviously useful on planes, trains, and automobiles to keep kids busy and engaged. But many of these games have an educational component such as language learning, math practice, or puzzle solving. You might download a bunch of free games that you expect your kids to enjoy, but wait to share them until you get to the airport. The games will be fresh and kids will begin them from scratch, making the most of their down time. Save some new games/videos for the trip home.

There are also plenty of apps for parents. Travel logistics apps can help you pack, convert currency, predict the weather, and translate languages. For getting around, most airlines have apps, as does Eurail. Uber is in many European cities now as well. Public transport systems may have their own apps, but often

Paris, France by Alexa, Age 13

all you really need is a good map, for which there are many apps (Google Maps is still awesome). Lodging can be found through big apps (TripAdvisor, Airbnb, Trivago) and small (Knok or apps from local apartment rental agencies). The app possibilities for restaurants are similar, although Yelp doesn't have a very big database in Europe yet. And getting local input for your itinerary is always nice (Spotted by Locals), as is a way to keep track of it all (TripIt). Happy surfing!

Count!

How can you encourage young kids to walk a long way or climb to the top of the tower? It's simple: just count. "Let's see how many stairs there are!" — and then start counting as you go. For slightly older kids, estimate in advance and then see how close the truth is to your estimate. The whole family can guess in the Price Is Right style — the winner is the person who comes closest to the real number without going over. Gambling (a close cousin of "The Ice Cream Bribe") is possible too and can empower parents to challenge whiny teens — and even reward them for a long journey. "If there are more than 300 steps, I buy everyone an ice cream cone. If there are less than 300 steps, you carry the daypack for the rest of the day." Exercise and pedometer apps on your smart phone can validate results.

TIP 43

Rome, Italy by Jordan, Age 10

Back-Pocket Questions

Carry a list of fun, observation-oriented questions in your back pocket, either figuratively or literally. It's pretty natural to ask kids "What was your favorite activity today?" or "What did you learn today?" but these questions don't prod thinking and many kids tend to shrug them off. A great question is "What did you notice today that was different from home?" or "What was different from a past destination?" Ask them to describe some of the people they met that day or list the new foods they ate. What do they think their best friend would think of the day's activities? Would their best friend like to be here? What would their grandparents like the most of all the things that they have done on the trip? How does the language impact the culture? Do these people tend to sound friendly? Smart? Happy?

Vienna, Austria by Zoey, Age 15

If you learned about a period in history or a particular event, ask the kids how that event might have shaped what they see on their trip. Often the kid-perspective isn't included in museum displays and history books, so ask explicitly about that. "What would it have been like to be a kid during World War I?" or "What do kids do for entertainment here that's unique?" Take a good look at a very elderly person and then imagine what they've seen in their life. Did they live through

TIP

44

a World War? Did they ever know Communism? What other kinds of changes have they seen in their life?

Mini-Fun

Down time on the road will present itself in unexpected places: while waiting for dinner, on a train, waiting for a tour to start, at a bus stop, in a museum café, or on a rainy afternoon with tired feet. Just as you're ready for down time at home with crafts, games, puzzles, and books, you'll need to be ready on the road. The only difference is that your supplies will need to be a lot smaller. Dedicate a one-gallon plastic bag to down time entertainment and keep at least some of it with you all the time. If you also plan to bring journaling supplies with you everywhere, you can manage with fewer additional activities.

TIP 45

Exactly what you bring along will depend on your childrens' ages and interests. Mini-coloring and activity books are great for a wide range of ages. Look for racks of Dover Mini Activity books at your local children's book or toy store (usually $1 to $2 each) or try searching an online bookstore for "mini activity books." Puzzle books and "grownup" coloring books for older kids are everywhere. Other craft ideas: mini crayon or pencil sets, tiny packages of modeling clay, stickers, multi-colored pens, stencils, felt shapes, blank white puzzle postcards, scratch art cards, or pipe cleaners. There's no need to lug it all around. Just tuck one small craft activity, for example 10 pipe cleaners, into your daypack each day. Kids will be more excited to find something new than to be presented with the same options day after day.

Key-chain sized puzzles are perfect and relatively easy to find. There are often very small toys such as plastic animals, plastic soldiers, or tiny dolls in the toy section of the drugstore. You can set these small figures up on any white paper placemat and sketch a house, zoo, farm, or outdoor scene. Add a small book, thin magazine, or a comic book plus a mini deck of cards to complete your "survive — and even enjoy— an hour anywhere" bag of mini-fun.

Brussels, Belgium by Leah, Age 7

Comparative Studies

As you travel from city to city, try picking a common thing to compare between places. It should be something that you're likely to look for anyway. The kids can compare hot chocolate (Bratislava is hard to beat), gelato flavors (there's gorgonzola in Florence), or spaghetti (the basic staple of many traveling kids). If your kid is going to order caprese salad whenever it's on the menu anyway, formalize the process by taking notes in a travel journal on the characteristics of each one. Maybe Italy won't have the best? Taking notes will help you remember the details from place to place. Parents can play with their favorite things too, like local beer or wine. But it doesn't only have to be about food; maybe compare the various ways you can pay to get on a city bus, the designs of sewer covers, or how many stray cats you see.

TIP 46

Neighborhood Playgrounds

TIP 47

European parks often have cool and exotic play structures that you won't find at home, and exploring them can be a regular afternoon outing in which your kids relax and recharge. You might discover a giant climbable art structure, a funky swing, or oversized jungle gyms. These all provide a respite from the slog of sightseeing. Try using Google Earth to explore a neighborhood near your lodging or ask a local where they take their kids. Be ready to divert from the day's plan when you come across a particularly interesting playground, or if you just need to take a break for the swings.

In many countries, "adventure play-grounds" are popular. These are open spaces dedicated to mud puddles, climbing trees, rope swings, hammers, nails, and fort-building. These often charge a small admission price and most are staffed. Your kids are also likely to find playmates at playgrounds, even though their only common language is an urge to play. Be alert to risky equipment as countries differ in their attitudes about liability and safety.

Granada, Spain by Ben, Age 14

Wear Their Shoes

TIP
48

nspired by Somerset Maugham's *A Writer's Notebook* and facilitated by your kid's travel journal and a little down time, try creating character sketches of people that you see on the street, at the market, or in the restaurant.

Use your imagination and create a fictitious life for someone that piques your interest. What do they do for a job? Who are their family? Where do they go for fun? You can prompt smaller kids with these and other questions, encouraging them to imagine how other people live and to be creative.

The kids might write the character sketch down in their journal or it can be the foundation of a family discussion about what life might be like in this place. Character sketches can help concentrate kids on what they've learned about the culture and how that might impact everyday life. Of course, be mindful not to make other people self-conscious because you're watching them. That can be part of the game.

County Mayo, Ireland by Caelan, Age 8

Snap It!

I f you're traveling with a teenager, this will already be obvious to you. You can use your cell phone to take a picture of anything you might need to remember or refer to. For example, take a picture of the public transportation map. Wondering which stop is next?

TIP 49

Just zoom in. Take a picture of the return bus schedule posted at the bus stop. Snap a photo of the menu selection you absolutely loved but might have a hard time remembering again. Snap a receipt or the name of a street that the helpful waiter wrote on your napkin. These photos serve as a reference and will trigger unique memories later. Maybe it's a timeline for the place, the Hapsburg Family Tree, or a list of the Kings and Queens of England. You could even snap a picture of a section in your guidebook or your three favorite tips from this book for later reference.

Budapest, Hungary by Zoey, Age 15

Deciding Where to Go & What to Do

Explore Real European Life

In Europe, you can visit monuments and icons that your kids will remember forever; show them art they will read about in college; and explore history in a more meaningful way than they can ever experience at school. You can also teach them about other cultures and other ways of living! Be sure to save time in your itinerary for the not-so-famous things, like grocery shopping, department stores, banks, post offices, and playgrounds. These can all provide a window into the daily life of people in a foreign country. You could also visit a small neighborhood off the beaten path, purposefully observe the subway system at rush hour, or choose to work out at a local gym.

Cultural Submersion

Swimming pools are a perfect place for literal cultural immersion. Not only do they provide a great opportunity for your kids to mingle with local kids, the differences between pools in different countries are often fairly dramatic and interesting to discover. In many countries, for example, the changing rooms are co-ed. In Austria, lap swim takes place without lane

Zurich, Switzerland by W, Age 2

lines. Very tricky! There are also lots of destination pools, known for views, architecture, or amenities. In Barcelona, you can view the city from the Olympic swimming pool, Piscines Bernat Picornell, way atop Montjuïc. On another day in Barcelona, visit Poliesportiu Marítim with four linked hydrotherapy pools, a lap-swimming pool, saunas, steam rooms, and a tunnel to the beach. What kids wouldn't enjoy, and even learn something, sampling swimming pools across Europe?

Get Lost

TIP 52

Most European cities were constructed before the dawn of the automobile and contain a core of winding streets and ancient buildings. These city centers are amazing havens for pedestrians. The small streets and alleyways are great fun for wandering and discovering. Make time for aimless drifting through these historic districts, often redeveloped as tourist centers. There may be street cafés, buskers, and small museums down a narrow alley.

Spending a few hours without the worry of automobile traffic can be especially relaxing for parents of young children. The best place in the world to wander until you are lost is Venice, where the canals and tiny bridges add an extra layer of intrigue. Wandering in Venice is even more spectacular in Biennale years, when there are international art installations around every turn.

Venice, Italy by Jordan, Age 10

Geek out

TIP
53

When most people think of European museums, they think of old buildings and famous art. But some of the world's best science museums are also here. Visiting one of these amazing museums will likely be a trip highlight. Not only will you receive a dose of scientific adrenaline, but you'll get a nice dose of European museum style. European children's exhibits are often quite special. Your family can check out science in the 18th century in London's Science Museum or burn off calories in the giant hamster wheel that's part of the bodyworks exhibit at Glasgow's Science Centre. On the outskirts of Paris, La Cité des Enfants within the Cité des Science et de L'Industrie is packed with hands-on activities.

The Deutsches Museum in Munich may not be on everyone's "must do" list, but it should be. The mind-boggling transportation exhibit includes a miniature railroad, over fifty planes in all different shapes and sizes, an interactive airport model, and a slice of a plane — a full, round slice of a Lufthansa airplane! And that's just one of the many exhibits. There's also natural history, communications, materials and production, energy, and musical instruments. Note that not all exhibits are translated into English but if you or your child want to learn about any of the topics covered in these exhibits, visiting the website before, during, or after a visit will provide all the necessary detail.

There are lots of smaller, science-themed museums scattered across Europe. These are often less crowded and full of discovery potential. Consider the Landek Park Mining Museum, an open-air museum on black coal mining in Ostrava, Czech Republic where guides are former miners. There's also the free Hellenic Children's Museum in Athens, Greece, with an extraordinary exhibit on the science of cooking. Soak up the new Muse in Trento, Italy, which combines stunning architecture with a focus on water and light. Wander into a three-story rainforest at the Universeum in Gothenburg, Sweden. Marvel at the Museo Nacional de Arqueología Subacuática (National Museum of Underwater Archaeology) in Cartagena, Spain. Did you even know that underwater archeology was a science?

How to Visit an Art Museum

Sooner or later you will probably want to take your kids into an art museum, and hopefully even enjoy the experience. No worries. All kids, from the very young to the very active, can have a blast on a trip to an art museum. First, set everyone's expectations, even your own. You won't get to see the entire collection at the leisurely pace enjoyed by art students or retirees. Prioritize what you want to see and do. Explain to the kids what you expect of them — quiet voices, no running, and a little patience. If possible, introduce them to the art you plan to see in advance through books and the internet. Explain why it is interesting. Also check YouTube for videos about the famous pieces you are most likely to see.

Once on-site, aim for a short, successful visit that leaves the kids wanting more. Definitely bring hands-on activities. Let small kids sit on the floor in the middle of the exhibit and doodle on white paper with colored pencils. Bring a sketch pad for older kids and offer ideas: sketch a painting that makes you hungry, carefully copy five different hands, sketch a famous painting but add three new details that make it better. Molding clay can add physical fun. Get a little silly with it by asking your child to create a miniature three-dimensional replica of a still life or the head of a person in a painting. Photograph the sculptural masterpieces, then smush them.

TIP

54

Paris, France by Alexa, Age 13

Allow kids to wear headphones and listen to their favorite music or to an audio book as they wander. Encourage restless kids to walk briskly, or to circle the perimeter of the room three times, scanning all the art to select their favorite piece. Once they've settled on a favorite, they can bring you over to see it or make you try to guess which one it is. You might create a simple scavenger hunt in advance. Include empty spaces for sketches, details to search for (a cat, a piece of fruit, a white horse, three styles of hat, etc.), and even word games (find something with the letter "z" in the name, find something that rhymes with "Fred," etc.).

If you really want to enjoy some slow art-gazing time, take shifts browsing exhibits alone versus wrangling kids. If there is a nice café, lengthen the trip with a refreshment break. Note that bribes are acceptable in art museums: "Visit two more rooms of paintings quietly and we'll get ice cream."

Be Advanced

Many of the most famous museums sell advance tickets online. This is a fantastic way to get ahead on a fun museum day, especially with impatient kids. The Louvre and Museé d'Orsay in Paris, the Uffizi Gallery in Florence, the Rijksmuseum in Amsterdam, and the Prado in Madrid all sell advance tickets. Beware, however, that advance tickets can be limited, so it's best to investigate months in advance or as soon as you have a firm itinerary.

TIP 55

Hit the Gift Shop First

TIP 56

Usually the gift shop is the finale of any museum visit. It may seem counter-intuitive, but sometimes it works best to start with what the kids want most. If the gift shop is always last, museums become something to endure — a necessary slog, undertaken only to get the treasure at the end. Try flipping the order. Visit the gift shop on arrival and let the kids pick out a treat. Now the kids have gotten their "needs" met and there is no incentive to rush through the exhibits. Try it! *(Tip idea inspired by Gillian SteelFisher.)*

Rub!

TIP 57

Grab a few large sheets of black paper and some thick rubbing crayons in metallic colors. Using these simple supplies and a roll of masking tape, create gorgeous rubbings of old and new objects all over town. For example, collect images of sewer grates from every city. Tape a large sheet of paper over an old grave on the floor of a cathedral and even young kids can capture a beautiful and unique image. Images of standing headstones are a little trickier but not impossible. Gravestone rubbings are allowed in many but not all places so you'll want to ask permission first if possible. You can also take rubbings of metalwork details, building plaques, or even leaves. Challenge your kids to find other textures that they can capture with this simple technique.

Public Transportation for a Sightseeing Tour

There are fairly expensive hop-on/hop-off bus tours in many major cities. These usually have audio guides in multiple languages that entertain you with fun facts and historical tidbits. Additionally, professional tour guides are waiting, pretty much everywhere, to take your family for a ride, literally and figuratively. Consider seeing the sights via public transportation instead. Public transportation usually connects all the major tourist hotspots and, in many cases, you don't even need to get off. For example, the Ringstrasse Tram Line in Vienna traces the path of a former medieval city wall. As such, it loops past dozens of impressive buildings, including the State Opera House and Hofburg Palace. You and the kids will want to get out and see some of the attractions, but you can enjoy riding by and looking out the window at others.

Porto, Portugal by LJ, Age 5

TIP

58

In Paris, try the #27 bus for crosstown sightseeing or the #72 for views of the Seine River. In London, the 11 route passes St. Paul's Cathedral, Trafalgar Square, the Houses of Parliament, and Westminster Abbey. Bonus, the kids can ride on the top floor of the double decker bus and get a great view! They have double-decker buses in Berlin too, and Bus 100 (red) goes right past Siegessäule (Victory Column), Bellevue Palace, Haus der Kulturen der Welt (House of the

Cultures of the World), Reichstag (German Parliament), the State Opera House, Bebelplatz, and Alexanderplatz. Obviously, the public "buses" in Venice, otherwise known as vaporettos, are a great bargain. Try Line 2 for a view right down the Grand Canal (in one of the two directions) or Line 12 for a locally priced trip to the outlying islands of Murano, Burano, and Torcello. *(Tip idea inspired by Camille Hubac.)*

Sewers Anyone?

TIP 59

Sewers can be pretty fascinating. Seriously. Several cities are so proud of their underground pipes that they run tours through them. Such cities include Paris, Brighton, and Vienna, which has a particularly popular sewer tour highlighting locations made famous by the 1949 classic Orson Welles spy film, *The Third Man.*

There are also tours in some small towns, but note that these may require advance reservations. Be ready for steep steps, grimy walls, and odd trivia. There are no guarantees on the quality of the tour aroma.

Ljubljana, Slovenia by Tonito, Age 10

Go Underground

TIP 60

Many churches went underground to store the bodies of the dead, either out of respect or to save space. In the cathedrals of Rome, Paris, Vienna, and Granada, as well as many others, you can explore musty tunnels to see underground crypts and rooms full of bones. Plan ahead because tours may not run daily or are held only at particular times. This is a spooky way to turn a typical church tour into something special.

Vacation Within a Vacation

People don't typically associate spas with family vacations, yet spas are not the exclusive domain of adults. With centuries of history as therapeutic centers, European spas have sprung up across the continent in any place that has geothermal activity. With just a little searching, you can find them everywhere, often with simple descriptive names like Bath (England), Baden-Baden (Germany), and Spa (Belgium).

TIP 61

Enjoy a lazy, luxurious day moving between cool, warm, and hot pools of mineral water at the historic Gellert Thermal Bath, Budapest. Spend some energy splashing and sliding at Wasserwelt in the Austrian Alps. Spas are awesome in any season, a great respite from busy traveling schedules.

Book It

A great deal of famous literature is set in Europe, providing iconic destinations likely to grab a kid's imagination. The 370-mile Fairy Tale Road in Germany links about fifty small towns and villages. Start in the quaint town of Steinau, home to the brothers Grimm, where a small museum sets the stage. Along the route, climb the tower at the medieval castle of Trendelburg where Rapunzel is said to have let down her hair. Then visit the 650-year-old Castle Sababurg where Sleeping Beauty slept peacefully for 100 years. If you're feeling a little extravagant, note that this is now a hotel. The road's finale is in the city of Bremen, where the Grimms' tale of musicians that outsmarted thieves is memorialized with statues in the town square.

TIP
62

Perhaps you're more interested in Hans Christian Anderson who once wrote:

To move, to breathe, to fly, to float,
To gain all while you give,
To roam the roads of lands remote,
To travel is to live.

Munich, Germany by Ilsa, Age 13

Visit the statue of The Little Mermaid in Copenhagen Harbor, the library in The Round Tower (also Copenhagen) where he wrote many stories, his childhood home in Odense (Denmark), or the interactive fairy tale museum in Copenhagen.

England has Paddington Station with a sweet statue of the bear himself. The Wind in the Willows museum in Henley-on-Thames, England, is a magical stop for small kids and parents too. It's hard to imagine that even hardened teens would not be charmed by the detailed dioramas, but if not, send them to the River and Rowing Museum upstairs.

There are a great variety of literary stops for older readers too. Fans of Harry Potter can find studio tours and amusement parks. With just a little digging, they can also locate real book or movie settings such as King's Cross Station, London, or the Glenfinnan Viaduct, Scotland. Tour the stunning and somewhat creepy Bran Castle in Transylvania, Romania, where Count Dracula is said to have lived. Or tour the Palais Garnier Opera House in Paris, home of the Phantom of the Opera. In England, visit Sherwood Forest in Nottinghamshire where Robin Hood is said to have stolen from the rich to give to the poor. The Major Oak, where he allegedly lived, is thought to be 800–1000 years old! Feeling even more literary? Visit the remains of Troy, Turkey, with your high schooler before she reads *The Iliad*.

Thou Learneth!

And in his brain,
Which is as dry as the remainder biscuit
After a voyage, he hath strange places cramm'd
With observation, the which he vents
In mangled forms.

TIP

63

Start in Stratford-upon-Avon where the Bard was born. Kids will enjoy visiting his house, a stunning piece of history in and of itself.

Costumed guides and period decorations create a vivid sense of life in the 1500s. *Shakespeare Aloud!* presents live performances on the property all year long, bringing his works to life. Next stop? A tour of the Globe Theater in London and perhaps a performance.

It is thought that Shakespeare never left England, but the settings for his plays define a terrific itinerary. Visit Kronborg Castle, a UNESCO World Heritage Centre, in Helsingør, Denmark. Stand under Juliet's balcony in Verona, Italy, and visit the nearby house attributed to Romeo's family. Of course, you'll have to visit Venice, ride in a gondola, and locate the hunchback on the Rialto bridge.

Many wonder how Shakespeare could have known about such details as that hunchback if he never traveled to Venice. In fact, there are seven years of Shakespeare's life that biographers can't account for. He was a father of young kids at the time. Could he have been traveling Europe with his children? As you travel, watch scenes from Shakespeare, find an outdoor performance, or read aloud. Don't expect to read a whole play with your kids, but a list of Shakespearian insults could keep a ten-year-old amused and entertained for hours. Great fodder for creative journal writing!

Who was Shakespeare anyway? A relatively recent book, *"Shakespeare" By Another Name*, is a well-researched biography of an Elizabethan poet-playwright named Edward de Vere, 17th Earl of Oxford, who some think was actually Shakespeare. Now this mystery makes the whole theme even more interesting! In the late 1500s, for example, Edward de Vere recuperated from illness in an inn at Windsor. Such an inn was the setting for *The Merry Wives of*

Strasbourg, France by Finn, Age 11

Windsor. Edward de Vere bought a house in Venice in 1575 and lived there for a year. In fact, his travels took him to many of the locations featured in Shakespeare's plays. Download "Shakespeare, The Google Earth Atlas" to follow the life and travels of Edward de Vere. Older kids can read the book. Everyone can puzzle on whether only a world traveler could have known the details in Shakespeare's plays. How would your kids solve this centuries-old mystery? A fun vacation in Europe can bring Shakespeare, whoever he was, to life.

Mix in the Modern

There have been a lot of great European artists since the Renaissance. Antoni Gaudí? Visit the Sagrada Familia Basilica and Park Güell in Barcelona, breathtaking examples of fantastical architecture that prove to be anything but boring for both kids and adults. Sketch it! Photograph it! Or just enjoy. Traveling with a college student? There's not a college dorm in the U.S. without posters of Salvador Dali's mesmerizing melted watches. Visit his home in Port Lligat, Spain (advance reservations required), or his self-designed mausoleum in the Dalí Theatre and Museum, Figueres, Spain. It is bedecked with giant eggs. Really!

TIP 64

In Vienna, seek out the buildings designed by Friedensreich Hundertwasser. And look for works of the famous Frank Gehry who designed amazing buildings in France, Germany, Spain, The Czech Republic, Denmark, Switzerland, and even Scotland. Modern architecture continues to flourish. Look up as you walk around! Most European cities have amazing modern buildings designed by architects you've never heard of.

Scholarly Wandering

E urope is filled with gorgeous old universities. Each has its own charm and most are unlike anything you might find at home. Top on most lists of beautiful campuses are Oxford and Cambridge Universities in England. Founded in 1167, Oxford University is the oldest English-speaking university in the world. Visit the spectacular Bodleian Library at Oxford University or the Wren Library at Cambridge University. If you're interested in the oldest university in the world, then consider a visit to the University of Bologna in Italy. It is also stunning, filled with red stone buildings, linked together by seemingly endless porticos. Other famously gorgeous campuses include the Sorbonne University, Paris, France; University of Coimbra, Coimbra, Portugal; Katholieke Universiteit Leuven, Flanders, Belgium; Wrocław University of Technology, Wrocław, Poland; and even the modern Freie Universität, Berlin, Germany. Enjoy your visit with younger kids by focusing on statues, gardens, libraries, cafés, and gift shops. Teens might enjoy a tour or be interested in learning a little about campus life. Everyone can have fun photographing stunning architecture, from whole buildings to small details such as a cornice, column, or roof peak.

TIP 65

Venice, Italy by Alexa, Age 13

Listen Up

Music is everywhere in Europe. It's usually good, and it's often free. It can be hard to find time for music and musical education at home, so take advantage of being a little less over-scheduled to listen a little longer. You can find street musicians in fairly predictable places and their performances are perfect for kids who can't sit still. Music is embedded in diverse cultural activities too. In Prague, there are hourly trumpet calls in the town square as well as trumpets announcing the changing of the palace guard. Church services may include beautiful music and many restaurants have live performances. Don't forget to give your teen time to explore the pop music scene.

Because of the rich musical history in Europe, music museums are relatively common. There is the Museé de la Musique in Paris where you can rent headphones that offer a guided tour including music samples. The Museum of Musical Instruments of Leipzig University in Germany houses over 10,000 objects including a great collection of piano rolls and a 1931 theater organ. You can "conduct" the Vienna Philharmonic Orchestra at Haus der Musik in Vienna. And, there is the small and eccentric Siegfried's Mechanical Music Cabinet in Rüdesheim, Germany, which displays 350 or so automatic musical instruments, from prototype jukeboxes to hand-cranked carnival machines to monstrous pianolas, all of which are in working order. As a finale, you'll discover hundred-year-old orchestrions — gargantuan wooden works of art that play all the instruments of an orchestra, including trombones and cymbals, at once.

TIP

66

Celebrate!

Consider attending a celebration. Witness an unusual religious festival such as Rouketopolemos. This translates to Rocket-War and is held at midnight the night before Easter in the town of Vrontados on the island of Chios, Greece. It's just like it sounds. Two rival churches shoot lighted rockets at each other in a spectacular battle streaking across the night sky. Walpurgisnacht, celebrated on the night of April 30th in Germany and under other names across Eastern Europe, combines traditions related to burning of witches, welcoming of witches, and the welcoming of Spring. Carnevale di Viareggio, held yearly in the small Tuscan town of Viareggio, Italy, with its gorgeous beachside parade of floats and masks, is held on several weekends in late February or early March every year.

There are secular celebrations too. La Tamborrada is a 24-hour drumming event in San Sebastian, Spain, in mid-January. The event dates back to the early 1700s and "sounds" like a lot of fun. If that's too loud for you or if you're traveling in summer, consider La Tomatina Festival in Valencia in August, a town-wide food fight estimated to consume over 10,000 kilos of tomatoes in exactly two hours. Or attend the Hay Festival held in Brecon Beacons National Park, Wales. The festival advertises itself as "a party where we celebrate the possibility of art, the adventure of science, and the deep understanding of humanity that comes from close attention to the lessons of history," and hosts events for children and young families as well as events for teenagers every year in May.

TIP
67

Be Festive!

Teens and brave parents can enjoy some of the best of modern music, from up-and-coming musicians to big-name stars, at one of Europe's many music festivals. Such festivals can be an amazing experience and also a wild ride. Roskilde Festival in Denmark, for example, is an eight-day event including over 160 acts. Most festival participants camp in giant, somewhat uncontrolled, tent cities. For size perspective, the festival draws about 160,000 people, including over 20,000 volunteers and 3,000 artists. Other big music festivals include Open 'Er in Poland and Positivus in Latvia. Smaller, and potentially more manageable, music festivals take place across Europe too. Examples include The Iceland Airwaves Festival in Iceland, and Fusion, in Romania. Denovali SwingFest focuses on experimental music and takes place in several locations.

Most of these music festivals are aimed at mature teens and young adults but others, such as The Latitude Festival in Suffolk, England, also include family-friendly events and activities.

Budapest, Hungary by Logan, Age 12

Vikings

TIP

69

The Vikings once ruled most of northern Europe. Originating from what are now Denmark, Norway, and Sweden, the Vikings went east to Russia, south to North Africa, and west to Canada. For 300 years, circa 1000, they were the European superpower. With that much history, you'd think that there might be some cool Viking museums out there, and you'd be right.

There's the Viking Ship Museum in Roskilde, Denmark, where you can not only see ancient ships that supported the vast Viking expansion, but also sail and row in modern replicas. At the Lofotr Viking Museum in Borg, Norway, you can visit

Copenhagen, Denmark by Ronan, Age 7

ancient building excavations and reconstructions, and even eat a traditional meal served by Vikings in costume. Birka is Sweden's oldest town, dating back to the middle of the 8th century. Now a UNESCO World Heritage Site, it is home to Viking archeological sites and historic reenactments. Bonus, it's a nice boat ride from Stockholm. There are Viking museums almost everywhere that Vikings went, so keep your eye out for them in England, Iceland, Germany, and Estonia.

Ancient Ruins

TIP 70

For most Americans, anything older than a couple of centuries is ancient. But in Europe, history takes on a whole different scale. Before the Modern Period, there were the Middle Ages, spanning the Renaissance, the Vikings, and the late Roman Empire. Before the Middle Ages, there was Ancient Greece and the Iron, Bronze, and Stone Ages. There are lots of ways to explore and even re-live these truly ancient times.

Stonehenge is perhaps the most famous prehistoric monument. You might also want to visit the Stones of Carnac, the Standing Stones of Orkney, and the Mound at Newgrange, all on the British Isles. Stonehenge is the youngest of these sites, dating from at least 2000 BC. If you'd rather explore what it was like to live in the Iron or Stone Age first hand, the Sagnlandet Lejre (Lands of Legend) open-air museum in Denmark allows families to immerse themselves for a week of reconstructed period living, complete with housing, food, and costumes. You become part of the exhibit, staying when everyone else goes home! There are similar stone-age museums in Finland, Austria, Germany, and the United Kingdom.

Athens, Greece by Jeffrey, Age 10

Palaces, Palaces & Castles

Many old European cities grew up around a castle on a hill. Budapest, Krakow, Prague, and Bratislava leap to mind, but that is just the tip of the iceberg. It would be easy to string together several months of travel just hopping from castle to castle. Of course each of them has its own fascinating story to tell, and all are beautiful in their unique and wonderful ways, but you want to avoid hearing your kids say "Oh no, not another castle . . ."

To break things up, try visiting one of the more strangely interesting castles.

TIP

71

On a warm summer day, there is nothing like the Wasserspiele at Schloss Hellbrunn outside of Salzburg, Austria. Developed by an archbishop with a "wet" sense of humor in the early 1600s, there are many dynamic water-powered dioramas, scenes, and statues that still work today and there are many opportunities to

be squirted when you least expect it. There's Predjama Castle in central Slovenia, built on the side of a cliff in the 15th century, making for stout defense and also providing a secret escape route through the caves below (which you can still visit today). And finally, Alnwick Castle in northern England starred as Hogwarts in the first two Harry Potter movies. One of some 1,500 castle sites in the United Kingdom, the 900-year-old Alnwick hosts period reenactments, Potter-themed performances, and even the occasional Tom Jones concert.

Hohenschwangau, Germany by Ilsa, Age 13

Old School Amusement Parks

TIP 72

I f you want your family to enjoy the thrills of a traditional European amusement park, head straight to Copenhagen. Right downtown you'll discover one of the world's oldest amusement parks, Tivoli Gardens, which first opened in 1843. Looking for the actual oldest operating amusement park in the world? Just a few kilometers outside of Copenhagen is Dyrehavsbakken ("The Deer Park Hill," commonly referred to as Bakken), which dates back to 1583. Don't let their ages fool you. Although both have dozens of classic rides and attractions, including old-school wooden roller coasters, there are also lots of state-of-the-art modern additions. These are great places to get your vacation thrill-ride fix and still enjoy a little cultural exploration and history.

There are plenty more classic amusement parks across Europe, both large and small. Barcelona is home to Tibidabo (reached via funicular), Prague has Lunapark, Berlin has Spreepark, and Vienna has the Prater. Norway's Hunderfossen FamiliePark is guarded by a 14-meter troll and boasts a giant fairy tale castle. Of course Paris has EuroDisney, but why bother?

Open-Air Museums

TIP 73

A n open-air museum is, as it sounds, a museum that exhibits stuff outside. Most commonly, these museums concentrate on traditional communities and ways of life. Displaying historic structures and recreations of past customs, these are sometimes also called living museums. Great examples include The Netherlands

Vienna, Austria by Zoey, Age 15

Open Air Museum (imagine working windmills), and The Open-Air Museum of Denmark. There is an association of European open-air museums (AEOM) with over twenty museums in a dozen countries, all focusing on bygone eras.

But an open-air museum can also describe a collection of sculpture, like Pedvale Open-Air Art Museum in Latvia where over a hundred sculptures are on display in a natural setting. Or it can describe unique architecture, like the Goreme Open-Air Museum in Turkey where church structures were carved from rock in the 10th to 12th centuries. There are also train museums, farm museums, and zoos, which, of course, have to be open-air museums too.

The Jewish Experience

The Jewish experience offers powerful lessons to which we should all bear witness. Jewish communities were segregated into their own districts in cities throughout Europe for centuries. The tiny walled town of Besalú, Spain, for instance, had a separate entrance for Jews in the 12th century. And, in 1290, Jews were banned from England, an edict that lasted for over 350 years.

World War II was the devestating culmination of this long history of persecution. Concentration camps provide the most potent example of the treatment of Jews by the Nazis. Dachau, outside of Munich, and Auschwitz, outside of Krakow, are both well-preserved remembrances of atrocities. Krakow is also home to a historic Jewish

TIP
74

ghetto, which is now a tragic echo of the thriving community that was decimated. Anne Frank's house in Amsterdam is a testament to the Jewish spirit. Note that these destinations require a large amount of mental preparation and education. They are likely too full of tragedy for young children and may even be more than otherwise-confident teenagers can manage.

A visit to the Zentralfriedhof (Central Cemetery) in Vienna offers a different window into Jewish losses. The cemetery is enormous, containing twenty-six bus stops! Tourists often visit the cemetery to find the graves of the many famous people buried there (Beethoven, Schubert, Brahms, the Strausses). The Jewish graves are segregated from the others and are worth a lingering visit. Although the non-Jewish graves are nicely manicured, you'll find many Jewish graves overgrown and in a state of disrepair. Why? Local families continue to care for the graves of their ancestors; however, the once vibrant Jewish community of Vienna was destroyed.

Lean to the Left

Europe has an extensive history of socialist policies, providing a perfect platform for an introductory conversation about comparative political science (it's never too early!). For details about Europe's socialist and communist past, visit the Museum of Communism in Warsaw, the Museum of Communism in Prague, or the Berlin Wall Memorial. Berlin is also home to the Museum Haus am Checkpoint Charlie where your kids will be fascinated by contraptions and disguises used to escape under, over, and through the Berlin Wall. In Budapest, send your teens to the House of Terror, which highlights the era's darkest aspects in a building that

TIP 75

was once home to communist-era secret police, or to the Hospital in the Rock, which displays the inside of a Soviet-era bunker. On a sunny day, there is no better place to marvel at political history than Momento Park, just outside of Budapest. At the park, you can wander amidst giant communist-era statues that were removed from Budapest after the fall of communism in Hungary in 1989.

What are the current hallmarks of socialist policies? There's the 35-hour work week in France, free university tuition in Denmark, and a publicly funded health care system pretty much everywhere. The City of Vienna is still Austria's biggest landlord as a result of housing complexes established during the socialist era. For a glimpse of what socialism has left behind physically, visit Karl Marx-Hof, the longest apartment building in the world with almost 1,400 units. Built in the late 1920s, the pink, modernist building has large courtyards containing playgrounds and kindergartens, and is decorated with proletariat sculptures over iconic arches that span city streets.

Ride the Cable

Frequently associated with alpine skiing, cable cars or gondolas provide a unique way to get around during all seasons. They are a fun and convenient way for everyone in the family to get from here to there. Ride a gondola all the way up to the Matterhorn from Zermatt, Switzerland, or visit Mont Blanc from Chamonix, France. At the top, you can enjoy lunch, a photo op, or actually ski. Those may be the most famous options, but there are cable cars strung across the whole of Europe that have little to do with the snow. Ride over the Thames in London, over the port in Barcelona, or swing for a 13.2-km ride between towns in central Sweden.

TIP 76

A funicular is a kind of cable car in which the cable is attached to two cars that move up and down simultaneously, counterbalancing each other. Unlike a gondola, which is suspended above the ground (sometimes quite high), a

Porto, Portugal by LJ, Age 5

funicular usually rides on the ground or in a tunnel. There are dozens of funiculars in Europe, usually providing access to hilltop castles (Budapest, Salzburg, Ljubljana), parks (Athens, Prague, Stockholm), or neighborhoods (Lisbon, Zagreb, Naples). You might also discover funiculars in funny places. For example, exiting Škocjan caves in Slovenia, there is a lovely funicular built right into a wooded hillside!

All Aboard

Europe boasts some of the most amazing train rides on Earth. Enjoy them not only for the transportation but for the experience. Consider the Jungfrau Railway in Switzerland, which leads from Kleine Scheidegg up to the Jungfraujoch at 11,332 feet above sea level! You'll travel in a tunnel for more than four miles on your way there. It's expensive (beware of cloudy days) but when else are you getting this close to the Eiger? Once you arrive, there are exciting things to do. Visit the ice palace or the Lindt Swiss Chocolate Heaven shop — probably the highest altitude chocolate shop ever! Also consider the Glacier Express or the Gornergrat Bahn, which both depart from Zermat and provide stunning views of the Swiss landscape. In fact, the views are so beautiful that the Glacier Express has attained

TIP 77

Vienna, Austria by Logan, Age 12

World Heritage status as a railway!

A one and a half hour trip on the Rauma Line from Dombås to Åndalsnes, Norway, will bring you up close to tall perpendicular rock faces and stunning bridges. The Flåm Railway offers spectacular views of Europe's longest and deepest fjord. The Bernina Express in Italy has loads of exciting tunnels and bridges. The Cinque Terre train from Levanto to La Spezia along the Italian coast is also a fantastic adventure. How about the West Highland steam line from Fort William to Mallaig in Scotland? The Hogwarts Express is said to be modeled after this awe-inspiring train. It's also only a one and a half hour ride. Wales has several "heritage" trains, including the Talyllyn Railway, a seven-mile narrow-gauge steam train that has been running since the 1860s and has been maintained by volunteers for over sixty years. In this same vein, there is the Strawberry Train from Madrid, the Šargan Eight in Serbia, and the Jokioinen Railway in Finland, among many others.

Boats, Boats, Boats

TIP 78

Everyone loves boats! And Europe is home to amazing boat possibilities. Cruise the Danube as guests on an organized tour. Or head out on your own by renting a long, skinny canal houseboat to explore the thousands of miles of canals and rivers in England, Scotland, and Wales. Just a night or two? Stay on a houseboat B&B in Amsterdam! Or try a floating hotel. Both the cozy Red Boat Mälaren and the white, full-masted af Chapman in Stockholm invite travelers to either hostel-style accommodations or private quarters.

Some areas simply demand boats. Greece, for example, consists of over a thousand islands. Ferry boats and sailboats are a way of life. Venice's charm, at least in part, is built on gondolas and gondoliers in striped shirts. If you want to witness even more boats in Venice, arrive for The Regata Storica in early September, which is preceded by a spectacular water parade. Visiting the fjords in Norway? Try a luxurious cruise or a paddle-it-yourself kayak.

There actually are a wide variety of paddling possibilities throughout Europe. England has its own fairly unique human-powered boats called punts. They are flat-bottomed boats found mostly along the Thames River and propelled by a five-meter-long wooden pole. Pack a picnic, rent a punt, and set out on a typically British one-day outing. You can also take your teens whitewater rafting on the stunning Sjoa River in Norway or arrange an overnight canoe trip down the River Obra in Poland.

Santorini, Greece by Jeffrey, Age 10

Sporting Options

TIP
79

Most of the famous professional soccer clubs of the world call Europe home and many offer summer camps for both kids and adults. St. Andrews, Scotland, is the home of golf and it's possible to play there if you reserve a year ahead of time. There's cricket, rugby, and volleyball; handball, cycling, and Formula One auto racing. All of these sports are played professionally and spectating is a good family fun.

There are also unique sporting events worth exploring. Calcio Storico, played during the third week of June in the Piazza Santa Croce in Florence, Italy, has been pitting rival districts of the city against one another since the 15th century. It's part rugby, part street fight. The pomp, ceremony, and noise are at least as much fun as the anarchy of the game. Also in Italy, the Palio di Sienna is a bareback horse race around the medieval Piazza del Campo of Siena that takes place on July 2nd and August 16th every year. Again, the pageantry of this event, dating back to 1656, is beyond anything your kids might find at home. Aside from bulls and tomatoes, Spain has *pelota*, a ball game of many forms. The basics of pelota are simply a wall, a court, and oftentimes wagering. There's a hand version, a racquet version, a basket version (*Jai Alai*), a Basque version, and a Valencian version. Switzerland has *Schwingfest* (wrestling), Estonia has *Kiiking* (extreme swinging), Romania has *Oina* (baseball/dodgeball), and the Dutch have *Fierljeppin* ("far-leaping"). People can make a game of almost anything.

Outdoor Scenery

The urban scenery of European cities can be spectacular, but the beauty of the natural landscape is also stupendous. On a big scale, there are mountains, forests, beaches, and seas. Your family can find tropical scenery or arctic scenery, high-elevation scenery or sea-level scenery.

TIP 80

Mountains, such as the Alps, Pyrenees, and Carpathians, are a central theme of many European countries, and you can visit during all seasons. Skiing is highly developed, with a couple hundred ski areas in Austria alone. There is a web of alpine huts that provide an amazing infrastructure for lightweight summer hiking, sometimes ski lift aided. Similarly, the Camino de Santiago is a centuries-old

Bergen, Norway by Gavin, Age 12

pilgrimage trail that terminates in Santiago de Campostela in north-west Spain. Though the popularity of the trail has skyrocketed in recent decades, it's still possible to find less well-traveled sections in small hill towns in France. And when you're in the mountains in the summertime, don't forget about the lakes and rivers. The Soča River in western Slovenia is particularly beautiful.

Beaches, at the other end of the outdoor scenery spectrum, literally ring the continent. Spain, Greece, and France all have famous beaches, and glorious beaches can also be enjoyed in Croatia, Denmark, and Ireland. Don't forget about the Faroe Islands and the fjords of Norway, mixing the natural beauty of both mountains and the sea!

Thar She Blows

No, not a whale . . . a volcano! Volcanoes aren't what most people think about when they think of Europe. Why not? Mt. Vesuvius made history when it erupted in AD 79 and buried the town of Pompeii near Naples, Italy. Visiting Pompeii now is an amazing archaeological experience, giving insight into daily life in ancient Greece. You might also consider a thirty-minute van ride to the base of the steep hike up to the crater on the mountain itself. The

TIP

81

Icelandic volcano Eyjafjallajokull, famous for more recent eruptions, is part of a stunning landscape. There's a small visitor's center and some exciting tour options (mostly suitable for older kids). Don't forget Sicily's Mount Etna, an active volcano with vistas of stunning black lava sand. You can hike to the top or ascend via cable car and 4x4 bus.

There are currently over sixty active volcanoes in Europe — the Stromboli volcano in Italy, Akyarlar in Turkey, Sousaki in Greece, and Kaiserstuhl in Germany, just to name a few. There are also many dormant or extinct volcanos. Visit the Chaine des Puys, a panorama of dormant volcanoes, cinder cones, lava domes, and explosion craters in central France near Auvergne. Make sure to save time for nearby Vulcania, a science-oriented amusement park with exhibits ranging from volcanic photographs to "Magma Explorer," an interactive expedition full of special effects. After visiting a volcano, take a few minutes to consider the role of volcanic eruptions in Europe's history. Maybe you really should think of volcanos when you think of Europe?

Spelunk!

Europe boasts a terrific assortment of caves. Kids (and adults too) love this stuff. Perhaps one of the biggest and most famous is the Postojna cave in Slovenia. Ride a 3.2 km train deep under the ground, explore stalagmites and stalactites, and observe Proteus, a pigment-free cave salamander commonly known as a human fish.

TIP
82
If your teen needs to go beyond traditional tourism, there are several varieties of adventure tours to choose from, including a tour of the cave system below Predjama Castle. You'll need to plan a few days in advance for these tours. Also in Slovenia, the Škocjan Caves are less developed and designated as a UNESCO World Heritage

site. When visiting caves, be sure to bring warm clothes and a flashlight. Be ready to experiment with photography too.

Caves aren't just for stalagmites and stalactites. Cuevas del Drach in Spain is home to a subterranean lake, Martel Lake, where classical music concerts are held daily. You can swim into the Blue Grotto, a sea cave on Capri, Italy or visit the Lascaux Caves in southwestern France to observe Paleolithic art estimated to be 17,300 years old. While the originals are not on view, an exact reproduction was created at Lascaux II with impressive guided tours. Watch *"Cave of Forgotten Dreams"* with your kids before you go. There are salt mines outside of Krakow where you can wonder at an underground church made of pink salt. Might as well also consider Wookey Hole in England, which boasts mini-golf, a circus show, a mirror maze, cave-aged cheddar, and more. You can even stay on-site in a family room at the Wookey Hotel.

Lunch Anyone?

TIP
83

I f you're eager to try some of Europe's famous fine restaurants, consider a lunch reservation. The menu will be similar, the prices cheaper, and you will get the experience that you might otherwise miss. Your kids are likely in an easier mood mid-day and the other lunchtime patrons might be a bit more patient than the dinner crowd. Bon appetit! *(Tip idea inspired by Bill Richards, Sr.)*

Carcassonne, France by Catherine, Age 8

Waiting for Dinner

Sitting at a table in a restaurant after a long day and choosing a meal from a mouth-watering menu of local delicacies is pretty fun. Sitting at that same table and waiting and waiting and waiting for the food to arrive is not so fun. Be ready with games! Young kids can play tic-tac-toe or dots on the napkin with a parent. They might also enjoy silly games such as Silent Simon Says. Have one person, "Simon," touch their nose and make a silly face or gesture (in silence). Everyone else has to imitate unless "Simon" doesn't touch his nose first. Word games such as Stinky Pinky can help pass the time too, especially if you're a little tired and punchy. Think of a pair of words that rhyme and have the same number of syllables — for example, fat cat, trouble bubble. Then give a two-word clue and let the audience guess or ask yes/no questions. For example, "overweight feline" or "dangerous sphere." Try telling the story of your day as a round robin with each person stopping either mid-sentence whenever they choose or every time a waiter passes by. Toothpick puzzles or riddles can provide hours of entertainment; look these up in advance. Teens may be more eager for civilized dialogue or a review of the day's pho-

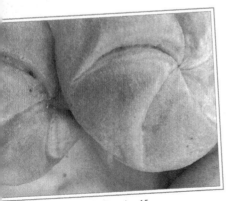

Vienna, Austria by Zoey, Age 15

tos but don't underestimate their need for entertainment when tired and hungry. Homemade versions of Scattergories or Pictionary can be perfect, as can a good old-fashioned deck of cards. Some days restaurant down time is best enjoyed with a nice book, a travel journal, or a simple sketch pad.

B.Y.O.S.

TIP 85

When traveling with small kids, it's okay to bring your own snacks or even whole kid meals into a restaurant. A fancy Italian restaurant might not seem like the right place to whip out cheese cubes and apple slices, but it really is okay. No one expected you to order a meal for your 18-month-old anyway. A happy, healthy, quiet child is much better for everyone than a cranky child without familiar food or a wild child hyped up on sugary snacks. Unwrapping complex items that require assembly or preparation is probably asking too much, so minimize the in-restaurant fuss.

Visit a grocery store or mini-mart and stock up on easy, healthy snacks such as single-serve yogurts, pre-cut fruits and veggies, energy bars, or pre-packaged snack meats and cheeses. You can also buy items in larger quantities, pre-cut them in your hotel room, and bring along manageable portions in plastic baggies. For a relaxing evening, venture off the beaten path a bit. The less the restaurant caters to tourists, the more likely it is that the staff will treat you with respect. Remember, most folks are pretty familiar with the universal necessity of feeding small kids quickly and healthfully.

Rotterdam, The Netherlands by Jaffer, Age 5

Batter On a Griddle

TIP

86

Authentic French crepes, Swedish pancakes, and Belgian waffles are special treats. Let your kids enjoy! In fact, there are variations of batter on a griddle across the continent, often associated with dessert though sometimes these delicacies are savory. Look for *tiganites* in Greece, *gaufres* in France, and *crempog* in Wales. The Swedes even celebrate Waffle Day (*Våffeldagen*) every March 25th!

Just Desserts

TIP

87

It probably wouldn't be the healthiest of ambitions to only eat desserts, but there is much more to the final dinner course than ice cream. Reward a good traveling day with a new and unique confection. Regional specialties give you and your kids a taste of local flair. Try *Kaiserschmarrn* in Vienna, a *trdelnik* in Prague, a Nutella crepe in Paris, and treacle pudding in London.

A tour of the unique and wonderful gelato flavors of Italy could be a trip theme all by itself. There are classics like cioccolato, stracciatella, and fruitti di bosco, as well as amarena, zabaione, and gorgonzola. Enjoy finding new flavors that you haven't tasted before.

Rome, Italy by Geneva, Age 13

Recording Memories

Travel journals are an awesome idea, but be careful not to turn them into a tedious chore. The only thing worse than having to write down every detail of your day is having to re-read every detail of your day years later. Instead, help your kids create a journaling habit based on reflection and creativity. Encourage them simply to describe their favorite moment of the day or give them a prompt such as "Ten Delicious Things I Ate on This Trip," "Other tourists I saw today looked so . . . ," or "I know I am in Germany because I can see . . . ."

On a day when you have a bit more down time, suggest that they write a short story set on location. On another day, they could draw a cartoon strip about something funny that happened. Most kids love to tape in receipts, postcards, museum floor plans, candy wrappers, and photos cut from brochures. Choose light, portable journals and keep them in a gallon-size plastic bag in your day pack. Add scissors, tape, colored pencils, and a nice pen. You'll be ready to journal wherever the mood hits or whenever you have a bit of time to kill. Re-reading these thoughts and reflections even years later will bring back images and ideas from the trip as well as great memories of who your kids were and what they thought about at that particular time in their life.

PART 3

HOME AGAIN

All too quickly after your plane lands at home, the joy and learning from a European family voyage can disappear into a whirlpool of carpools and homework. It doesn't have to be that way. The tips in this last section of the book will help you and your kids keep the trip alive even after you return home. They'll help in reinforcing what you and your family learned on your adventure, in rediscovering your own backyard, and in maintaining a traveling spirit.

Making Memories Stick

Party Time!

Coming home is fun, but it can also be a big let-down. In either case, the memories will slip away quickly when subjected to back-to-school shopping and friends who aren't particularly interested. Hang on to your memories with a party! The party might be as simple as having a few friends over for dinner or it might be a big, themed fiesta. Pick out recipes online that represent your travel destination or different parts of your itinerary; make it a potluck with a destination theme; or order take-out from a nearby ethnic restaurant connected to your recent trip. Sometimes fun drinks from various destinations can be an easy no-cook highlight. Check European food stores, Cost Plus World Market, or even liquor stores. High-end liquor stores often sell exotic mixers that are hard to find anywhere else. Make a centerpiece out of your travel souvenirs. Be prepared to share candy from your trip as a kid-friendly dessert. During dinner, ask your kids to share their favorite memories and ask your guests for their favorite travel memories too. It doesn't have to be *all* about your recent trip. You could also stick silly conversation starters at every seat such as "What was the worst thing that ever happened to you on a trip?" and "If you could go anywhere in the world for one month, where would it be?"

Toplice, Slovenia by Viviana, Age 10

After dinner, take a few minutes to let your kids share their travel journal and show photos. No need to torture your friends and family with 3,467 photos, each explained in excruciating detail. Pick a very small sample for sharing and discussion. Can your kids be ready to tell your guests about what these photos describe? Since you are likely to have zillions of other pictures, drop those into a slide show that advances automatically and leave it running during appetizers and dessert.

Display Your Travel Booty

TIP 90

While it is tempting to tuck everything away as you unpack it from your suitcase, it's also nice to leave it out. Set up a table or a special shelf to display the souvenirs, trinkets, collectibles, and even the travel journals. Pick a place where your kids are tempted to look over the items and where visitors will easily notice and comment. A big windowsill? A living room display table? The goal isn't to show off or to gloat but rather to keep the trip fresh in your memories as well as to open up interesting conversations in which your kids can share their stories and learn from the travel stories of others.

Caherdaniel, Ireland by Lillie, Age 8

Share With the Class!

TIP 91

Travel is not only an education unto itself, it can also enrich formal education. If your kids are in preschool or elementary school, encourage them to give a short presentation to their class about their trip. Help them put together a PowerPoint presentation with a map describing the itinerary, a few photo highlights, an anecdote or two, and maybe a few fun historical facts. Help your child rehearse and remind them that it's always best to leave the audience wanting more. A little show and tell can add to the fun. If possible, share candy or treats that you hand-imported. Everyone loves Swiss chocolate! Or make a special treat for the class from a country you visited such as Austrian *Marmorgugelhupf*, Portuguese *Cavacas*, or Swedish *Hallongrottor*. Families who plan ahead could send postcards back to the classroom at regular intervals or photograph a favorite stuffed animal at every icon.

Chat with older students about how their European experiences connect to their schoolwork. World War II? Mozart? The double-helix shape of DNA? There might be an opportunity for an extra credit report but, more likely, just some fun dinnertime conversation and perhaps a good excuse to watch a few old movies together, such as *The Third Man*, *Amadeus*, or NOVA's *Secret of Photo 51*.

Keep Up the Geography

TIP 92

After a family trip, your kids might be particularly inspired to learn a bit more about European geography. Any facts they soak in will certainly help give context to their middle school social studies material or their AP World History course. Try playing "10 Days in Europe," a board game based on mapping a travel itinerary by plane, sea, and foot across Europe, or "Get Ready to Ride," a beautiful train game also set in Europe. Want something your kids can play while waiting in line at the grocery store? There are a host of fun and educational apps for learning geography. Consider GeoFlight Europe or TapQuiz™ Maps for geography quizzes your kids (or you) can play like video games. A big floor-size puzzle can be fun, or leave a detailed little European map puzzle out on the kitchen table. You might also choose to go for an old-fashioned wall map with your route highlighted in colored yarn. Add pins for places you want to go next.

Bring the World Home

TIP
93

There are a zillion possibilities for cultural education without leaving your living room. Now that your kids have gotten a taste of travel, help them keep sampling different countries or dive in and explore one country in depth. Head back to the library to explore nonfiction books or ask the children's librarian about fiction set on-location in your child's favorite city. *Faces*, a magazine for kids dedicated to cross-cultural explorations, often has stories about kids in Europe and always has great features on kids around the world. Travel magazines aimed at adults can also be fun for kids because the colorful photos will invite memories and travel dreams. Explore *Bell'Europa*, dedicated to travel in Europe, or *Wanderlust*, an independent British travel magazine. *Bringing the World Home: A Resource Guide for Raising Intercultural Kids* by Dr. Jessica Voigts and Lillie Forteau is packed with ideas for music, video, dance, crafts, and more to enrich an evening, a playroom, or the whole house and to keep newly discovered European cultures alive.

Develop a Pen-Pal

Yes, it's possible to e-mail, post, tweet, and snap, but letters, written with an ink-filled pen on an actual sheet of paper, still have a special meaning. Help your child enjoy this activity with some nice stationary, a few printed pictures,

Greece by Jeffrey, Age 10

and ideas about what to write. They could write a letter to a family or child you met *en route* or you could locate an enthusiastic pen-pal via friends or friends of friends. A quick search online using "finding pen-pals" yields dozens of sites that offer to match up kids in one country with kids in another. What on Earth should they write? Describe a typical day in school, make a map of their neighborhood, explain the customs of a recent holiday, tell about their weekend. And they should ask a few (just a few) specific and related questions to keep the conversation going. While writing is slow and messy compared to typing or social-networking, receiving a letter back in the mail with real stamps on the outside is a timeless pleasure. Paper letters can be saved and re-read over and over again. Perhaps make a quick scan or photo copy of your child's outgoing letter before it is sent and then compile a folder to collect the letters to and from in chronological order.

TIP 94

Take a Mini-Trip!

Europeaxcursions don't always require a plane ticket. Pick a country that is well-represented in your home town, and explore it through art, food, culture, and film. Take out a few books on your "destination" from your local library to set the mood. These could be fiction or nonfiction. Look for a unique local cultural opportunity such as a dance performance, an art exhibit, a cultural festival, or a music event. With younger kids, work in an age-appropriate craft and print out coloring sheets such as the flag, the map, or a person in traditional dress. Choose a restaurant or a recipe that features food from your "destination" — have an explorer's mindset here and really try something different and new. If you are eating at home, make sure to play music from your destination and talk about current events. Finally, watch a film. It's pretty easy to find appropriate foreign films for teens. You can often purchase them cheaply or stream them from the internet. Children's films are more difficult but absolutely possible. Just search up "best foreign films for kids" and see what new and wonderful lists are available.

For example, a "trip" to France with young children might include waking up to crepes, visiting the Impressionist's gallery at the local art museum, relaxing in the café, coming home to paint flowers in the garden, sampling cheese blind-folded, cooking *boeuf bourguignon* while listening to Edith Piaf, and winding down for the evening by watching *The Red Balloon*, a peaceful classic children's film. For teens? Ask them to learn a bit about French politics for dinner discussions, choose the cheese for the blind-folded taste challenge, learn a traditional French game to teach to the younger kids, and, of course, dare them to try *escargot*! Try watching *The Extraordinary Adventures of Adèle Blanc-Sec* with teens or, better yet, encourage them to choose a film themselves.

TIP 95

Discovering Your Own Backyard

Take an Outsider's Perspective on Your Own Home

TIP 96

During your days and weeks in Europe, you and your kids were outsiders. Some information was easy to find and other information was really difficult to discover. You needed a map, ideas of important landmarks to visit, and cultural information to make sense of your surroundings abroad. Now that you're home, you can use that outsider perspective to gain new insights about your own neighborhood, city, or culture by working together to design a visitor's guide. Start by creating a map. What are the important landmarks for your child? What does he or she think are the most important landmarks for visitors? Landmarks might include schools, a coffee shop, an area of significance in family history, public art, friends' houses, or the orthodontist office. Give older kids a bigger area such as your entire city or the nearest small town and task them with identifying cool spots that adults don't know about or things a teenager needs to know to ride the bus.

The second stage is a little trickier. What are the stories about your town or the activities that might interest a visitor? What neat things have happened in your town? These don't have to have national or international significance, but perhaps there is a house that was rebuilt after a major fire. Perhaps there

Salzburg, Austria, by Ilsa, Age 13

is a native tree species that is unusual and a particular park where this species of tree can be observed? Is there an ugly statue that has a funny back story? Make a short list of local stories and destinations for your next visitor and add the important locations to your map.

Lastly, think about a few tips that visitors might need to know to understand your local culture. These might be hard to identify at first but they are usually really fun to think about. For example, visitors to Seattle might need to know that locals never use umbrellas. Visitors to Boston might need to know that the sprinkles folks put on ice cream are called "Jimmies." Young children will be surprised to discover what is unusual about their hometown. Before they traveled, they assumed every place was just the same. Now they can identify and appreciate unique bits of their own culture from their new perspective. They might choose to create a cultural guide for your home. It could include a few basic rules that visitors need to know like "We never feed the dog scraps from the table," or "Everyone has to wash their hands before they eat." If there's enough interest, decorate a three-ring binder and put the map, destination list, and cultural guide inside. Place it on the table by your guest bed.

Search Out a Festival

ultural festivals are a way to unite a local community based on shared heritage as well as a way to share traditions with new people. For your family, they give you a chance to keep in touch with one or more of the cultures you visited and learn about the cultures near your home. Many cultures have special festivals. A festival might be as simple as a few booths in a rented hall or as complicated as a multi-day party held in a big event space. The Festival

TIP

97

of Nations in Saint Paul, Minnesota, for example, collaborates with over 100 ethnic groups including, in past years, groups from Poland, Germany, Italy, and Slovakia to provide an incredible multi-day event. Also look for events that focus on just one culture such as FinnFest USA, an annual multi-day, traveling event.

Community colleges and universities as well as neighborhood centers and language schools are good places to search for cultural festivals. These events may be advertised poorly outside the target community so search online, look for Facebook groups, or ask friends. Before the festival, chat with your kids about what they remember and what sort of traditions, products, or foods might be represented. Then enjoy reconnecting with Europe while discovering the cultural richness of your home.

Invite an Exchange Student Into Your Home

Hosting a guest from another country for an extended period will teach you and your kids a great deal about the guest's country as well as a great deal about your own country. Exchanges can be formal or informal arrangements. Make sure you set up a situation you can trust, either through a formal agency, a community organization, or friends. You'll want to set expectations in advance as to whether the exchange student will have any responsibilities such as childcare, cooking, or teaching a foreign language.

TIP

98

County Clare, Ireland by Brenna, Age 10

And also be clear on how finances for vacations, outings, restaurants, and groceries will be managed. You might want to cover some basic ground rules such as alcohol, curfews, and dating. With a little preparation, most exchanges are very successful. They will enrich your family's daily routine and give you a great excuse to cook new foods, explore your own city, and practice a foreign language. They might even bring a life-long friend into your child's life.

Be a Tourist in Your Own City

Enjoying a traveling spirit doesn't necessarily mean leaving home. There are surely unexplored corners of your own or a nearby town. But visiting a new place isn't quite enough. Capturing the traveling spirit might take a little more than an afternoon outing. First ask yourself and your family what, exactly, makes traveling so special. Is it really the museum exhibit or is it being trapped on a train trying to find entertainment? Ingredients of a satisfying day of travel might include navigating a bus schedule, enjoying a leisurely lunch, walking until your feet hurt, staying out a little too long, and taking silly pictures. Much of this can be captured right at home if you can manage to block out a whole day on your calendar. Head out by local bus to a new museum or an area with art galleries, walk to a new restaurant, take in a show and grab an ice cream cone on the way, then navigate home again by bus. Play restaurant games, try to see familiar places with a fresh perspective, take pictures on the bus, and don't worry if you get a little lost. Encourage reminiscing about your European adventure or a little dreaming about your next destination. Being an adventurous and enthusiastic tourist, even for just a day and even without actually leaving home, can be a great antidote for the stresses of real life.

TIP 99

The 100th Tip
For Traveling
With Kids
In Europe

Rome, Italy by Jeffrey, Age 10

Travel Time Is Family Time   TIP 100

Travel Time Is Family Time

Your visit to the Eiffel Tower, your dinner at the expensive restaurant, or your tour of the art museum will not be the measures of whether or not your trip was a success. In the end, a European vacation will be about the family memories and traditions you build together and the open-mindedness and multicultural enthusiasm you develop in your kids. You will be trapped in a small hotel room, negotiating every meal, navigating twenty kinds of transportation, enduring heat and crowds, and simply being together 24/7.

This is your golden opportunity to get to know your kids and grow family memories. It's your time to share ideas about politics and history, to people watch together from a park bench, to listen to your kids as they observe strangers, and to try new foods that turn out to be delicious (or disgusting — it doesn't really matter). The Eiffel Tower is not worth a horrid, all-day meltdown. Eating too much ice cream or skipping out of the museum early to race to the beach are the memories you'll savor most.

London, England by Jordan, Age 10

Epilogue

I f you find that these tips are fun and useful, grab a copy of our first book, *Family on the Loose: The Art of Traveling with Kids*, also published by Rumble Books. Organized into the same three parts as our 100 Tips, *Family on the Loose* details even more ideas for getting the kids excited, customizing your travel logistics, packing light (with reproducible packing lists for the whole family, including packing by pictures for non-readers!), designing

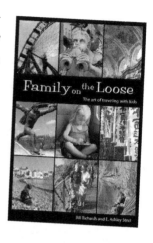

kid-centric daily routines, and extracting the educational from any experience.

With a more global perspective, the book is crammed with informative sidebars, such as craft ideas to prepare for common destinations, tips for getting "bumped" off a flight, and quiet activities for the plane ride, plus it includes creative reproducible pages for city scavenger hunts, making budgets, visiting a museum, and imaginative journaling. In fact, there's an entire chapter on creating the world's best travel journal with fill-in pages you can copy and tape into your child's journal to get them started. We also provide plenty of fun suggestions for keeping the traveling spirit alive when you're back home.

Zaandam, The Netherlands by Jessica, Age 13

Acknowledgments

We are once again indebted to our editor, Amanda Elkin. She made every tip a little better and a lot more fun to read. We learn something every time we get her edits back. Matt Mayerchak and Laura Glassman brought the tips to life with their playful design ideas. Their attention to detail and patience with our schedules and corrections made the whole process a pleasure. Amazingly, we have yet to meet Amanda, Matt, or Laura in person. We are so lucky to have found these wonderful long-distance partnerships.

We thank our friends for their patience with book talk and, especially, Ben and Stacey for digging through old photos to find just the right ones. Caroline encouraged her kids to send photos from the road and provided enthusiasm for this project all along the way. Friends and family also inspired us with terrific tip ideas that make the book better.

Many virtual friends also took the time to locate photos taken by their children on past trips. We thank wanderingeducators.com, thepiripirilexicon.com, kidstravelbooks.com, kidworldcitizen.org, evavarga.net, thevacationgals.com, irelandfamilyvacations.com, kidsareatrip.com, momvoyage.hilton.com, and pintsizegourmets.com. We are deeply thankful for everyone's trust and for their willingness to jump in and help bring a true kid-perspective to our project. The photos make the book so much more than just our words could do.

This book would not exist without our family. Our kids have embraced the traveling spirit and the value of multiculturalism in everything they do. They've encouraged us, been patient with us, and made every trip more fun. Our parents shared with us these same values of adventure and multiculturalism. We are both grateful for road trips and plane trips when we were very young and for all that our parents taught us along the way.

About the Authors

E. Ashley Steel, Ph.D., and **Bill Richards** have traveled to over forty countries and have two wonderful and well-traveled daughters. As a family, they have lived in or visited the United States, Canada, Asia, Central America, Eastern Europe, Western Europe, and the United Kingdom. After writing this book, they hope to meet more people who, on returning from the great European family vacation, have taken time for a kid's museum and a swimming pool.

Ashley is a research scientist specializing in river ecology and statistics. She spent many summers teaching science to kids at a University of Washington academic summer program, leading students on eccentric adventures to undiscovered corners of campus. Her published science curriculum, *The Truth About Science* from NSTA Press, has sold over 5,000 copies. Her travel bug was ignited by frequent trips to England as a child and her enthusiasm for travel only grew during a college semester in Denmark. She has since been honored with a Luce Fellowship for a year in southern Thailand, and a Fulbright Fellowship to live and work in Austria.

Bill is an accomplished forest ecologist, specializing in restoring forest habitat for rare wildlife species. His work has appeared in the *Natural Areas Journal, Conservation Biology,* and *Forest Ecology and Management.* Bill grew up on both sides of the U.S.-Canadian border and accompanied his parents to over a dozen countries before graduating from high school. He has since lived and worked in Australia, Thailand, and Austria, and has traveled extensively in Central America, Eastern and Western Europe, and West, Southeast, and East Asia.

Venice, Italy by Logan, Age 5

Colophon

A note on the type:

Text is set in Minion Pro and Myriad Pro. The handwritten font is Pea Andrea from www.kevinandamanda.com.

This book was designed by Mayerchak + Company. www.mayerchak.com

Cover photos and dedication photo were taken by Bill Richards, Ashley Steel, and Lillie (age 8).

Valencia, Spain by Ben, Age 14

Made in the USA
Lexington, KY
18 November 2017